INSURRECTION

INSURRECTION

What the January 6 Assault on the Capitol Reveals about America and Democracy

★ ★ ★

John Rennie Short

REAKTION BOOKS

Published by
REAKTION BOOKS LTD
Unit 32, Waterside
44–48 Wharf Road
London N1 7UX, UK
www.reaktionbooks.co.uk

First published 2024
Copyright © John Rennie Short 2024

Printed and bound in Great Britain
by TJ Books Ltd, Padstow, Cornwall

A catalogue record for this book is available from the British Library

ISBN 978 1 78914 841 1

Contents

Insurrection

1. the action of rising in arms or open resistance against established authority or governmental restraint . . . an armed rising, a revolt; an incipient or limited rebellion.
2. the action of rising up; upheaval.

Oxford English Dictionary (1961), vol. v, p. 364

The alternate domination of one faction over another, sharpened by the spirit of revenge, natural to party dissension, which in different ages and countries has perpetrated the most horrid enormities, is itself a frightful despotism . . . The disorders and miseries, which result, gradually incline the minds of men to seek security and repose in the absolute power of an individual; and sooner or later the chief of some prevailing faction, more able or more fortunate than his competitors, turns this disposition to the purposes of his own elevation, on the ruins of Public Liberty . . . the spirit of party are sufficient to make it the interest and the duty of a wise people to discourage and restrain it. It serves always to distract the public councils and enfeeble the public administration. It agitates the community with ill-founded jealousies and false alarms, kindles the animosity of one part against another, foments occasionally riot and insurrection.

George Washington's Farewell Address, 1796

You can call it an insurrection or you can call it a war or fight.

Elmer Stewart Rhodes, Leader of the Oath Keepers,
November 2021

Preface

January 6, 2021, Washington, DC. It was a cold, cloudy, gray day. The beautiful days of fall had passed, the deep cold and winter storms of late January and February were still to come, and the cherry blossoms of March and April that adorn the city were still months away from flowering. The day started off cold, around 40°F at first light. Winds from the west kept the temperatures low all day, and it was only around 42°F at noon when Donald Trump, the 45th president of the United States, stood on a platform specially constructed for the event on the Ellipse just south of the White House. He spoke to a crowd of supporters, between 10,000 and 15,000 people who had assembled from around the country, obeying his call to action. He told the crowd and the audience watching on live television that the recent election was stolen: "They rigged it like they've never rigged an election before . . . we will stop this steal." He reiterated his 77-day-long messaging that the election of November 2020 had been stolen from him by radical Democrats, big tech, and the media. It was a typical Trump speech filled with lies and deceptions, self-aggrandizement and puffery, outrage, meanderings, and just plain bluster that only occasionally came into sharp focus when he exhorted his followers to action: "Because you'll never take back our country with weakness: you have to show strength and you have to be strong." He mentioned Mike Pence by name because of a mistaken belief that the vice president had the ability to refuse to certify the results of the election. Near the end of his speech, he exhorted his assembled followers, "And we fight. We fight like hell. And if you don't fight like hell: You're not going to have a country anymore . . . So, let's walk down Pennsylvania Avenue."[1]

★ ★ ★

Even before he finished the speech, some of Trump's supporters were already walking eastward along Pennsylvania Avenue and the Mall toward Capitol Hill, where a joint meeting of Congress was assembling to certify the election victory of Joe Biden. Hours later, some of his supporters broke into the Capitol, disturbing the proceedings in an act of insurrection that sought to overthrow the outcome of a legitimate election.

There are multiple causes for any significant event. There are the long-term and the short-term, the hugely influential and the merely tangential. Some are known. Some are half-understood and many remain unknown. Some may be the inevitable consequence of things years or even decades in the making, some dependent on happenstance, change, and contingency. It is difficult then to provide a neat and simple explanation for the events of January 6, 2021. Dramatic events, especially historic ones such as the storming of the Capitol, occur at a distinct time and specific place, but their origins like a spiderweb take time to mature and cast their influence.

The anthropologist Clifford Geertz, drawing on the philosopher Gilbert Ryle, outlined the idea of a thick description to go beneath the surface appearances. This book is an attempt to provide a thick description of the insurrection, to uncover the deeper roots and the underlying structural causes including the belief that individual rights always trump community norms, a sense of White entitlement, and the cult of violence that runs through u.s. history as a deep river of blood. I attempt to tell a story of how the United States drifted into the dangerous political moment where established politicians as well as significant numbers of the public raised doubts about the results of a legitimate election, encouraged and shared conspiracy theories, and gave support to those who would tear down democratic institutions. The wider story includes the loss of trust in government, a legitimation crisis, growing polarization, and the normalization of extreme ideas and disruptive political agendas. These issues were turbocharged by the events of the last few years, including the covid-19 pandemic, crises of policing, and a racial reckoning a century in the making. Place, as well as time, was also a factor. The unique role of Washington, DC, as the nation's capital, with its distinctive governmental structure, also came into play. There are many threads to this web. Rather than the breathless account of an insider sharing rumor and gossip, this is an account of how recent events emerged from longer-term processes.

★ ★ ★

Insurrection focuses on four issues: two long-term processes that unfolded over decades and two shorter-term events that came into full force in 2020. The long-term trends are a loss of trust in government (Chapter Two) and a mounting democratic deficit (Chapter Three). The two shorter-term events of 2020 include the covid-19 pandemic and the long, hot summer of social unrest (considered together in Chapter Four). Chapter Five pivots to a discussion of the recurring importance of conspiracy theories in the United States and the consequent politics of outrage that helped to fuel the insurrection. Chapter Six focuses on the presidential election of 2020, immediate responses to the election results, and an attempted coup. Chapter Seven examines the immediate events of January 6, 2021. Chapter Eight considers the aftermath of the insurrection and the long-term implications for the health of the Republic.

A longer summary, Chapter One, highlights how Trump managed to capture the base of the Republican Party, and maps how his presidency progressed from a small lie about the crowd size at his inauguration to a raging river of mendacity, and ultimately to the Big Lie of a stolen election.

Chapter Two discusses the reasons behind the popular discontent with government in the United States. I draw a parallel between Trump and his immediate predecessor. Although widely contrasting in many ways, they were both insurgent candidates who were brought to the presidency via popular sentiment—a voting public that believed the existing political structure was essentially bankrupt. I explore the idea of the legitimation crisis in the United States and posit reasons for this crisis: the hollowing out of the American middle class, the disruptive effects of globalization, the enthronement of financial capitalism, and the stark generational differences within the u.s. population.

Chapter Three assesses the mounting deficits of u.s. democracy that have contributed to disillusionment with the system and politics more generally. Numerous sources are considered: the power of money, the Supreme Court, congressional representation, gerrymandering, voter suppression, the Electoral College, and state suppression of local progressive initiatives.

Chapter Four uncovers the roots of what I term "the politics of outrage," in the politicization of media, especially in the aftermath of Federal Communications Commission rulings in 1989 and 2011 that allowed overtly political speech, the 2010 midterm elections that transformed the political landscape, and the rise of the Tea Party. The narrowing of news context to partisan commentary, and especially the rise of Fox News, led to the marketing of opinion and prejudice instead of analysis. Trump's unfiltered Twitter tweets were part of the viral nature of social media communication. The outrage was amped up in order to mould audiences into believing that *others* were a source of disruption, disorder, and treason. It was us vs. them.

Chapter Five examines the 2020 events that fed into the insurrection: the pandemic in its early stages, when state mandates for lockdowns created a populist backlash, and the social unrest in the racial reckoning in the wake of George Floyd's death. Mask mandates were interpreted as a transgression of individual rights, and so fueled a surge in a literal, populist call to arms by the gun-toting Right. The social unrest often resulted in popular protests, which in turn attracted right-wing militarist and racist groups. The long, hot summer of civil unrest created a fertile environment for the insurrection.

Chapter Six focuses on the presidential election of November 2020, and looks back to previous electoral debacles—Gore and the hanging chads—that led to a lack of faith in the election process. It explores the operation of the state regulation of federal elections, while focusing on the steady drumbeat of Trump's claims that the election result was always going to be rigged and his second term of the presidency stolen. I concentrate on how the result was framed before, during, and after the election.

Chapter Seven returns to the scene that was first presented in Chapter One, taking the narrative from the end of Trump's speech to the march on the Capitol. It describes some of the main actors involved and briefly discusses how DC policing is so very different from that of other American cities. Several key themes arise, including the importance of armed militia on the fringes of U.S. political discourses, the demonization of political opponents, and the constitutional complexities of an event that captures the unique position of Washington, DC, caught as it is between city, state, and federal policing. There are many reasons behind the failure to protect the Capitol, but this chapter concentrates on the structural factors that made January 6 such a fiasco for security forces.

Chapter Eight considers the aftermath of the insurrection in terms of how it is being understood and explained by different groups in the United States, and evaluates what it could represent for American elections to come as well as for the future of the Republican Party. Could we see a return to normal politics in the United States? I suggest that the insurrection marks an inflection point. While the United States maintains a military superiority over most nations in the world—although China is rapidly closing the gap—its soft power was seriously devalued by the Trump presidency, the insurrection, and the Republican response. The final chapter, by its very nature, is more speculative than the previous seven, since it attempts to peer into the future and answer a pressing question: does the insurrection signify the end of the democratic experiment of the United States?

1

From the Small Lie to the Big Lie

It began with a small lie and ended with the Big Lie, which in turn led to a coup and then an insurrection.

The Small Lie

In the United States, presidential elections are held in November of election years, and the new administration is sworn into office two months later, in January, at a staged inauguration ceremony. It is a legacy that follows from when people moved by horse and carriage, transport was slow, and it would have taken weeks or even months to assemble a new Congress. The inauguration itself is held on the grounds of the Capitol. The ceremony formerly took place on the East Front of the building, a large plaza of open space bounded by white marbled buildings, the Capitol to the west and the Supreme Court and Library of Congress to the east. For his 1981 inauguration, Ronald Reagan moved the ceremony to the West Front, where it has been held ever since. Compared to the more limited public space outside the East Front, the West Front—with its steep facade—looks south across the much larger public space of the 2.6-mile Mall stretching past the Washington Memorial to the Lincoln Memorial.

In 2009, the inauguration of President Obama took place on January 20. The bitterly cold day did not stop a record attendance. The crowd stretched from the steps of the Capitol to beyond the Washington Memorial. It was the first time the entire Mall had been opened up to the public. The *Washington Post* estimated the crowd size at around 1.8 million.[1] There was documentary evidence from satellite imagery and cameras on the ground to show that it was the largest inauguration crowd in presidential history.

Eight years later, to the day, in 2017, Donald Trump took the oath of office. The day before the inauguration a Fox News poll revealed that only 42 percent of registered voters had a favorable opinion of him, while 55 percent felt unfavorable toward him. The avowed populist was not all that popular. These numbers did not move much throughout his presidency, only cratering at its very end when a Gallup Poll during his last week in office showed one of the lowest approval rates on record for a sitting president.

January 20, 2017, the day of his inauguration, is now best remembered for two events. The first was a brief speech when he was sworn in as the 45th President of the United States, on the steps of the very building that four years later he would direct his followers to march on. He spoke about an America of abandoned factories, economic insecurity, and rising crime. It is often referred to as the "American carnage" speech, in which Trump described an America of inner-city poverty, crime, drugs, and "rusted out factories scattered like tombstones across the landscape of the nation." It was a dark vision, a story of decline that Trump promised to reverse. "That all changes," he declared, "starting right here and right now."[2]

The crowd size was estimated at between 300,000 and 600,000—large, but less than one-third of the number for

Obama's first inauguration. The second event took place the next day when the White House press secretary, Sean Spicer, the first of four to take the role during Trump's single term of office (a national record) who later became a much-mocked figure by late-night television comedians, stated that it was the largest crowd ever to witness an inauguration. He went on to claim that the media estimates of a small crowd were false. He did not speak the truth. At the time, it seemed such a needless, stupid lie. It was easy to check the visual images from satellites, a process made all the easier because the National Park Service, as part of a plan to rejuvenate the grass on the Mall, had laid down white sheeting to protect newly planted grass, thus inadvertently making the pockets of absence far starker on screen. The records of mass transit on the day of the inauguration, eyewitness accounts, and photographic information all pointed to a less than record-breaking crowd. Trump told Spicer to lie, because, well, it was easy to lie, there was no real cost to the lie, and, more significantly, his ego required, indeed demanded, a larger crowd than Obama had received. When questioned about the veracity of the press secretary's statements, the president's counselor Kellyanne Conway said that Spicer was merely presenting "alternative facts."[3] The Trump Presidency as it turned out was based mostly on alternative facts. That small lie was just a taste of things to come over the next four years.

Alternative Facts

It was a little lie and in the scheme of things not all that important. It was so obviously false. It remained an inside-the-Beltway story with little traction outside the capital, but it signaled the start of an attempt by Trump to impose his will on the national conversation. The effort to create a reality that promoted Trump, despite facts to the contrary, was nothing less than an attempt at the "cognitive capture" of the public discourse to bend the common understanding of reality to what Trump says it is, rather than what it is in truth. The cavalier use of easily checked lies as the truth was an act of power, as if truth itself was what the president alone decided. In effect, the aim was to suggest that something could not be a lie if the president had said it as fact. Truth was not an objective condition, confirmed by multiple observers. Rather, truth was what the president said. In this creative redefinition of the truth and cavalier use of "facts," it was perhaps the first truly post-truth presidency. Friedrich Nietzsche noted that there are no facts, only interpretations.[4] Whichever interpretation prevails at a given time is a function of power and not truth. The Trump presidency and its attempt at cognitive capture was truly a Nietzschean will-to-power.

★ ★ ★

At the start of his tenure of the highest office in the land, many hoped Trump would grow into the presidency. The trajectory was in the opposite direction. He turned the office into a projection of his personal whims, anxieties, and insecurities, strange fixations, and recurring obsessions. With vast presidential power released from the commitment to distinguish truth from falsehoods, the Trump Administration and its supporters created an alternative reality aided by an army of Twitter trolls, Fox News commentators, and a Republican Party that seemed immune to any facts that disrupted the narrative of Trump as a great president. Outlandish claims, denial of plain facts, distortion, and lies became standard.

These were not just small fabrications or minor slip-ups in veracity, but the attempted cognitive capture of an entire political discourse. Such activity was an assault on the very assumptions of modern life, as if the Enlightenment had never happened and the Scientific Revolution was a failed coup attempt. Rationality itself started to float away from its traditional moorings in the u.s. body politic.

The tiny trickle of the "small lie" turned into a huge tide of mendacity. The *Washington Post*'s Glenn Kessler regularly publishes a record of the lies of politicians. He estimated that President Trump made more than 30,000 false claims in little over four years. He lied about the big and the small; he lied about his enemies and sometimes even about his friends. He lied about his economic record and even cures for covid-19. In speech after speech, tweet after tweet, and interview after interview, he made baseless claims, told outright lies, and promoted patent falsehoods. He doubled down on lies that were exposed. He kept claiming he presided over the most successful economy, he was the best president, the biggest tax cutter. Other presidents had lied or promoted falsehoods, too, but Trump's mendacity was on an industrial scale that beggars the imagination and clearly tested the ability of the mass media to respond. In a single day alone, November 2, 2020, as he electioneered across the country, he made 503 false or misleading statements. The lies mounted, and culminated in the Big Lie about the 2020 presidential election.[5]

Trump and the Media

The mainstream media had an intimate relationship with Trump in his meteoric rise to the presidency. During his first presidential campaign, CNN acted like his own official channel. His appearances and speeches were given lavish coverage. Sometimes CNN showed images of an empty stage and a lonely microphone to signal that Trump was about to speak. The CNN coverage was often uncritical and rarely called out candidate Trump for the mistruths and lies. The head of CNN, Jeff Zucker, had a history with Trump: Zucker was previously an executive at NBC, the station that commissioned Trump's hit reality show *The Apprentice*, which boosted the network's ratings. The show made Trump a household name and solidified his image with many viewers as a successful, savvy billionaire with sharp business sense. Later, when Zucker moved to the top job at CNN, he helped to elevate Trump to national prominence. It was a transactional relationship. Zucker used Trump to boost CNN's ratings at a time of tough competition from MSNBC and Fox News. Trump, in return, received the equivalent of billions of dollars in free publicity. He called himself, accurately as it happens, a ratings machine, and was proud of the fact that he could boost viewership and readership. The relationship deteriorated, however, once Trump came to power. CNN slowly reformed its coverage but by then it was too late.

The veteran broadcaster Jake Tapper, a CNN anchor during Trump's rise to the presidency, felt, like many commentators and television journalists in the mainstream media, that his role was simply to present the arguments of Trump and the other candidates on the assumption that it was the viewers and readers who had to make their minds up, without undue influence. When confronted early on about his lack of rigor in covering Trump, Tapper replied that it was up to the audience to perceive the lies and falsehoods. It was not the media's role, he argued, to intervene in the relationship between the president and the public.[6]

In the early days of his presidency, the mainstream media still clung to an outdated notion that, even in the face of lies and falsehoods, they had to be evenhanded in their coverage. The mainline media response of so-called balance—on the one hand Trump says "this," and on the other, critics say "that"—clearly failed to cope with asymmetric falsehoods on such a mass scale. It was the equivalent of a science show that, for the sake of "balance," has someone who says the world is round, and another who argues the world is flat, and the moderator allows both to stand unchallenged in the interest of "fairness." There was no serious reckoning of the lies that spilled over and polluted the national discourse. At the beginning of his presidency, there was so little critical investigation by the mainstream news that the distortions and alternative facts gained traction and oxygen. There was an abject failure of public news media by outlets seemingly in thrall to the carnival-like atmosphere of Trump's presidency and their growing audiences and increasing revenues. Trump was a money machine for the media.

Trump's lies were reinforced by Fox News, the Republican Party, cabinet ministers, celebrities, newscasters, friends, and business associates in a superstructure of mendacity that supported the president. In the early years of the Trump presidency a spineless, self-serving media allowed Trump to push the boundary of false narratives further and further so that by late 2020 he could claim that the election had been stolen—and more than 70 million people believed him. By then, mainstream media had adopted a more critical position. But it was too late. The well of truth had been poisoned and discourse so polluted that many Americans had a hard time telling truth from fact and honest brokers from mountebanks and charlatans. When even basic facts are questioned then the door is opened to the unscrupulous and the self-serving.

Without a shared narrative or even a shared sense of reality, the United States had separated into different "truth" communities.

Trump didn't always have an intimate relationship with Fox News. The principal owner, Rupert Murdoch, had an ambivalent attitude towards him. Fox was not an early supporter of Trump's candidacy, and he was even taken to task by Fox reporter Megyn Kelly at the Republican Party presidential debate in 2015. But Murdoch realized that there was an overlap between Fox viewership and the Trump base. Commentators crafted their delivery to both create and appeal to that base. Fox News became Channel Trump. Trump called into live shows and was given a platform, and commentators were giving chances to signal their close ties with the president and gain legitimacy with their audience. It was not a one-way street. Influential political talk news hosts and commentators at Fox such as Maria Bartiromo, Tucker Carlson, Lou Dobbs, Laura Ingraham, Jeanine Pirro, and Sean Hannity also played major roles not only in favorably reporting on Trump and gaining solid audiences in the process, but in having a huge direct influence on Trump himself. People who interviewed well on their shows could sometimes end up with a position in the Trump administration. This key group of Fox news commentators had direct access to Trump, forming, in effect, a cable news cabinet, even suggesting campaign strategy and tactics.[7]

There was a successful symbiotic relationship between Trump and Fox News. The president had a firm media ally and was assured of positive media coverage. Fox News in turn increased ratings with its privileged access to the president. As Fox News and Trump hugged each other in a tight, uncritical embrace, other networks sought to carve out a separate and distinctive niche. MSNBC, for example, attracted viewers who wanted more critical coverage of Trump. Near the end of the Trump presidency media coverage was seen to become more critical, prefacing remarks typically with, "In an unfounded claim that has no legal support, the President claimed that the election was stolen." However, this more assertive reporting alienated Trump's bedrock support even further from the mainstream news. Trump's continual use of "Fake News" became the shorthand notation for *the media lies about me, you cannot trust them. You can only trust me. I alone have the truth. Believe me. Always believe me.* And many did.

Trumpland

The Trump presidency was like nothing that came before. Let's begin with Trump himself. Trump had always been challenged by an impartial truth. He had a fervent belief that what he thought was true or what he wanted to be true was really true despite all evidence to the contrary. Alternative views to his were not just wrong, they were lies, deceptions. They were fake news. His ego could not handle being wrong, mistaken, or seen as a loser. Self-aggrandizement was and is his way of being in the world. Self-reflection, self-doubt, and self-deprecation were not identifiable traits of his personality. The Trump self was unreflective, undoubting, and profoundly ego-centered.[8]

It is important to remember his business background as a private business real estate developer. He developed the special skills required to create buildings from nothing, to persuade banks to lend huge amounts of money while working through the always complex and sometimes corrupt legislative and regulatory jungle of city, state, and federal governments. The real estate business is built on ambitious plans where gleaming towers are imagined from abandoned sites and new office blocks are conjured up from former waste dumps: It is a sector where developers take on huge debt to finance speculative ventures that in effect are giant leaps of imagination. The speculative real estate sector is as much based on fantasy, longings, and dreams as on careful costings, specific plans, and precise engineering. It combines the spectral and the real, the imagined as well as the actual. In his ghost-written biography, *The Art of the Deal*, Trump alluded to the fact that his business model was based on playing to people's fantasies. It takes magical thinking, enormous self-confidence, no countenance of failure, a willingness to bend the rules, and a relentless commitment to strike a deal in your favor. Trump brought these skills to the presidency. Like a speculative developer selling a new luxury hotel built on a former waste site, he sold an image of an America that had been polluted by previous administrations that he, and only he, could make Great Again. He promised a big, shiny, new building of an America Made Great Again. His presidency was the property developer's credo writ large: Bend the truth for personal advantage. He shaped and reshaped the public discourse and recreated the political norms and public culture almost at will, coming to capture and dominate not only large parts of the political establishment of the Republican Party, but a large sector of the electorate.[9]

Trump grew up in a world of privilege and entitlement. He made his money the most reliable and old-fashioned way—he inherited it from his father, a successful real estate developer and landlord in New York City. He took over the family firm in 1971 and ten years later renamed it the Trump Organization. Much was made, especially by backers and supporters in his later political career, of the idea that he was a successful businessman, but this was more myth than fact. In reality, his business ventures always teetered on the edge of legality and the verge of bankruptcy. He faced thousands of legal actions and his company was involved in six bankruptcies between 1991 and 2009. He continued to face difficulties even when he diversified from risky real estate to the franchise model that used his name to brand various ventures. Trump had to pay $25 million in damages to settle a civil suit and two class actions against the claims of those who were defrauded by Trump University.[10]

The image of the successful businessman and corporate titan was burnished further by his appearance on the successful television show *The Apprentice*, which first aired in 2004 and ran until 2015. For fourteen seasons Trump was presented as a powerful CEO. But he was not a successful businessman, he just played one on television, and he played the role very well. With his tall frame, big hair, and supreme self-confidence, he fit the picture of what many people imagine a successful businessman to be. In the show, contestants were divided into teams and charged with completing various tasks around New York City, such as starting a business. The culmination of each episode was Trump, in a hypermasculine-themed boardroom, assessing the participants and announcing to one, "You're fired!" The popular show created an image of Trump as a commanding force, decisive, a natural-born leader. More than 27 million people watched the finale of the first season. The television show did more for his reputation as a powerful businessman than his actual business career ever had—a business career that was, for all intents and purposes, entirely unfitting for a future president.

There are different types of business organizations. Trump was not a CEO of a public company subject to oversight and scrutiny by shareholders and a board. He was the head of a family firm whose employees owed their primary allegiance primarily to Trump himself. There were no internal critics of Trump or of his behavior—he was the boss and patriarch of a firm that favored nepotism, with cronies and children seeded throughout the organization. The arrangement suited and reinforced his paper-thin sensitivity to criticism.

Trump carried this business experience into government. He turned the presidency itself into a larger version of his family business—for one thing, he brought both his daughter and son-in-law into the White House in advisory roles—and as an extension of himself, unencumbered by oversight and distanced from criticism. The presidency, like the Trump Organization, was reconstrued as a mechanism of his personal will, with the government and the Constitution merely extensions of his personal power. He imagined himself not as a servant of the public, bound by norms and long-established conventions, but more as the unchallenged leader of the most powerful company in the world, the u.s. government. His bromance with Russia's president, Vladimir Putin, was built on his envy of the Russian leader's seemingly unbridled personal power and strongman persona.

Trump's popularity was also a product of the cult of celebrity in an age of social media. Trump was well known long before he became president; his role on *The Apprentice* had increased his profile and celebrity status, and he was firmly part of the well-populated landscape of second-tier famous people. Social psychologists have noted that social media can be used by celebrities to attract a loyal following. Followers create "parasocial" bonds with their chosen celebrity which are especially nurtured by constant messages, tweets, and likes. Studies have shown that for people who share Trump's ideology, reading his Twitter feeds makes them feel like they know him personally, as if they're reading a friend's or friend of a friend's tweet, and so like him even more. One study further suggested that the format of *The Apprentice* allowed people to create strong parasocial bonds with the host, and those who established such bonds were more likely to vote for Trump in the 2016 election. These parasocial ties widened and deepened during his presidency. This explains the curious fact that a man so lacking in empathy could establish such a strong bond with his supporters, many of whom idealized and idolized him. They genuinely felt that they had established a close relationship with Trump, as if he could understand them and feel their anguish and pain. The television star who played a success became a success, while picking up a solid base of idolizing supporters.[11]

Trump had a significant presence on Twitter before becoming the U.S. President, but after he was elected, his tweeting gained greater visibility and diffusion, and his tweets increased in number and intensity. Online social networks are now major circuits of political ideas and beliefs. Social psychologists at New York University found that in the online universe, the stronger the emotive language used, the greater the impact. Moreover, the stronger the moral and emotional language employed, such as anger, disgust, and outrage, the greater the diffusion. This contagion effect can be applied to Trump, as his more emotive tweets have always been the most liked and most retweeted. Trump mastered the world of social media and knew, perhaps instinctively, that the more his tweets expressed anger and resentment, the more they spread. Trump's base of supporters was widened and nurtured by the diffusion of his emotive language on social media. Like a viral contagion, anger and outrage became the currency of political discourse. Trump set the pace, character, and terms of the debate. He was the accomplished master of the 24-hour news cycle.[12]

Only six months into the Trump presidency, I half-jokingly referred to "Trump Fatigue Syndrome," or TFS, writing in July 2017:

> I have just been diagnosed with an illness, TFS. It is injurious to long-term health and perhaps too early to say whether it is fatal . . . It is caused by overexposure to President Donald Trump. Its symptoms include a depressing sense of watching the same drama over and over again. And just like being stuck in a movie theater watching a badly scripted and poorly produced B movie, it begins with feelings of exhaustion, then panic, with the realization that it may never end.

And what was the cause of this syndrome? Well,

> All diseases have vectors; the carriers of this disease are the mass media of both left and right political persuasion. They cover Trump endlessly because it generates more viewers and listeners. The presentations are suitably tailored to appeal to their respective audiences. Trump the hero of the forgotten Americans on Fox News. Trump the political incompetent on CNN. Trump generates money for the networks whatever their position. He makes news and attracts viewers through constant controversies. The President provides all the tweets, images, talking points, and general mayhem: all the media has to do is to roll the camera

and queue the talking head panels. For the mass media Trump is the equivalent of easy money; for the audience, the equivalent of empty sugar calories that produce a buzz but not much substance. In the Age of Trump Fascination there's no need to send reporters on overseas missions or do deep reporting about what ails the Republic and its peoples. The cheap and easy coverage of Trump allows us to imagine that we are engaged in political debate or critical analysis while in reality we are just party to a flimflam show masquerading as the u.s. presidency. All diseases have symptoms. For those on the left there is a rising sense of exasperation about what the President does and speaks. Outrage is continually aroused, leading to exhaustion. For those more to the right there is a feeling of resentment against the antipathy to their President. Again, outrage is continually aroused, leading to exhaustion. Most diseases have cures. We should begin our diagnosis with the realization that we no longer inhabit a Republic of political debate but a squalid banality of neo-reality television. This fever of constant outrage will have to be purged or it may kill us all.[13]

A lot has been written about the authoritarian tendencies of Trump. For some, Trump represented a threat to the Republic, and hypercritical commentators often drew parallels with fascist dictators. "Is Donald Trump a Fascist?" was a frequent question for discussion. There were some resemblances: the cult of the leader, the ethnonationalism, the nurturing of the sense of grievance and victimhood among his supporters, the othering of immigrants and minorities, the allure of violence. And there were the rallies. Rallies were the stages for the rants of Hitler and Mussolini and were a vital part of the theater of European Fascism. The term "rally" was rarely used in the United States outside of the formal political campaign season. But as the season of electioneering turned into the "eternal present" and Trump came to love the rallies as a way to connect with his base, the rally became a regular feature of his presidency. Adoring crowds would wait for hours to hear him speak and listen raptly through the long, meandering speeches. His performances contained not the white-hot anger of Hitler, but more the theatrics of Mussolini, with the same repertoire of strutting and gesturing, ironic facial poses, and the intense personal communion between leader and followers. But direct connections with fascism misdirect our gaze to a European past. In fact, the Trump presidency was a profoundly American event of the present, rooted in the realities of the contemporary United States. To be sure, it had parallels with other countries at other times and we can learn much by looking at similar contexts of social dislocation and disruption, but it is best understood as an American phenomenon. The "is he a Fascist?" question can lead to a misunderstanding of the Trump regime, imagining it as the import of a foreign ideology rather than rooted in the American present.[14]

Comparing Trump to totalitarian leaders misses the point. Trump was more of an authoritarian. The German social psychologist Erich Fromm, in trying to make sense of the rise of Hitler and the Nazi Party, described an essential dilemma for humans in the modern age: whether to embrace or escape from individual freedom. To embrace freedom in the modern world was to inherit uncertainty, insecurity, and a life of constant questioning. For many, escape is the easier route. And it can take a variety of forms, from conformity—the subjection of one's individuality to community norms and ideals—to destructiveness, to giving up control to someone else, most notably the Great Leader, who can provide a sense of historical determination and permanence, and offer a comforting national narrative. German intellectuals such as Fromm, Herbert Marcuse, and Theodor Adorno—all trying to make sense of the fall of Weimar and the rise of Nazism—argued that the authoritarian character can emerge at times of great social and political upheaval as people seek order from chaos, permanence from transitoriness, security from precarity. In the contemporary era, Fiona Hill makes the point that economic decline and the associated socioeconomic disintegration can lead to persistent disadvantage, and lack of opportunity that can in turn lead to an authoritarian populism. She describes the process at work in multiple locations, from northeast England to Russia and middle America.[15] Trump was the embodiment of the authoritarian tendencies in contemporary American society. The embrace of Trump was not a deliberate step to totalitarian fascism but an escape from uncertainty and insecurity. The slogan *Make America Great Again* was not a fascist rallying call; it was the primal scream of insecurity seeking a solution in authoritarianism.[16]

Much has been written and said about Trump's personality. The long-standing "Goldwater rule"—which counseled experts to avoid making clinical statements about politicians, or others, based only on their public persona—was routinely broken. Trump's was a personality too big and too public to be ignored. In 2016, the psychologist Dan McAdams described Trump's personality as a toxic mixture of sky-high extroversion and grandiose narcissism.[17] Another study suggested that, even compared with other abrasive, narcissistic, and confrontational political figures, Trump was an outlier.[18] There is a limitation to most of these studies, coming as they do from "experts" who have not fully examined or counseled Trump. Those willing to make the diagnosis at a distance tend to have pre-existing anti-Trump positions, so the results are less than surprising. However, a triangulation of the varied accounts from insiders, journalists, and others suggests that Trump has a narcissistic personality that reacts strongly to any sense of failure or criticism. From the various sources, though we must be ever mindful of their agendas and biases, it is possible to assemble a picture of Donald Trump: a man who imbibed a toxic positivity from his father and thus carries with him a need to be perceived by others as a winner—never, ever, a loser. He is very susceptible to flattery; he is impulsive, distrustful of experts, and relies on his gut instincts almost to the point of instability; he is a narcissist who could not distinguish between his own self-interest and that of the country he was elected to lead—for him, they were one and the same thing. Trump has little regard for the consequences of his rhetoric and actions, and is disinterested in facts. He was often bored by the work of being the president but enjoyed the rallies where he could connect with his supporters and control the narrative of his presidency, the duties of which he often showed himself to be unprepared for. He had little regard for objective truth. He was morally compromised and ethically challenged. A dominant trait that played a huge role at the end of his presidency was that he could never admit to being wrong and would ultimately do anything to avoid being seen as a loser. Losing was a form of death to the Trump ego and had to be avoided at all costs, even to the Republic.[19]

In effect, Trump created an alternative America. Let's call it Trumpland, a land filled with supporters, funders, and followers, true believers, and those with an eye to personal advancement. Its population came from an America that is older, whiter, more evangelical, angrier. It contained the poor and the wealthy tied together by a grievance that the country was changing and for the worse. They fear the Other, sometimes defined as Black, LGBTQ+, immigrant, or foreign-born. They feel threatened by science and disturbed by critical evaluations of the United States and its history. Theirs is a lazy nationalism that sees America only as a source of celebration, subject neither to debate nor criticism.

Trumpland had its own national history devoid of racial subjugation, inequality, and racial injustice. It was filled with anger and frustration, its people bitter about their inability to obtain wealth and feeling that the American Dream has been undermined by migrants and refugees from outside the country's borders. America is great, they exclaimed, but being taken advantage of. In a stunning rhetorical twist, the richest, most powerful country in the world was described by many of its own people as a victim. Trumpland had its own cast of characters but only one currency, unrelenting support for its leader. He even showed comradeship with Nazi demonstrators and insurrectionists simply because they supported him. His need for adulation allowed him to dismiss the evil ideology and motives of those who wanted to live in Trumpland.

At the center of Trump's inner court was his family, especially his two sons, daughter, and son-in-law, who all gave him advice, trading on his name, monetizing their family name and their access to him. There was an outer court filled with a revolving group of people, as secretaries of state, attorney generals, and secretaries of defense came and went, pushed out in part because they failed to provide enough support to Trump.

Any hint of disloyalty, more so than incompetence or corruption, eventually led to dismissal. The outer court knew the rules of the game.[20] What was required was not only allegiance and loyalty, but the outright signaling of that loyalty. One of the more revealing scenes from the Trump presidency was a cabinet meeting in which discussion moved around the room with each cabinet member praising the president.[21] It was more fitting for a meeting chaired by Stalin or Kim Jong-un. The only member who refused to go along with the charade was the then secretary of defense, a marine and an army officer of many years, James Mattis. He resigned his post in December 2018 and subsequently described Trump as a threat to the Constitution.[22]

Trumpland also provided home to extremists who had been denied entry to the Republican Party. Trumpland, like all self-respecting countries, had its own media and news service. There are the organizations, such as Fox News, that like *Pravda* to the Soviet Communist Party were loyal mouthpieces. And then there are the multitude of other outlets, the Facebook communities, the podcasts, and websites of the conspiratorial, the outraged, and the obsessed. At times, Trumpland seemed like America on crack and heroin. Hyperexcited, passionate, angry, tribal. It was home to those who felt they had no voice. Trumpland was a haven, a place that gave purpose, relevance, and meaning to those who felt denied all of these in mainstream America. For the citizens of Trumpland, "lamestream" America was unable or unwilling to see the existential and looming threats to the United States. Trump was not only their leader. He was their savior.

Like all presidencies, Trump's was marked by failure and success. His greatest personal and Party failure was his inability to expand support beyond a narrow base. The base held firm, but he could not break through to majority approval. The public's approval rating, according to Gallup, hovered around 41 percent, dropping as low as 34 percent and only reaching as high as 49 percent. A mash-up of numerous polls suggested an approval rate of around 40 percent and a disapproval rate consistently above 50 percent, peaking at 55 percent during the summer of 2020. His failure to extend beyond his support base cost him politically, and ultimately lost him the 2020 presidential election.[23]

His interest in the presidency was more performative than administrative. He enjoyed the rallies and marches, the pomp, and the presidential circumstance of the office. He was lax in his more mundane duties and seemed to spend most of his time either golfing, watching Fox News, tweeting, or chatting with cronies and friends; at times he seemed only marginally concerned with actually doing the job of president. He basked as the stock market rose but refused to take any responsibility for its fall in the wake of the COVID-19 pandemic. He promised an end to endless wars, but U.S. troops still remained in Afghanistan. His presidency was more successful in giving tax cuts to the wealthy and reducing regulation of businesses and environmental polluters. He failed the big tests of government, such as dealing effectively with the pandemic. He seemed disengaged, unconcerned, and at times totally oblivious to the trials of ordinary Americans. His main concern was an unrelenting and laser-like focus on his own image, how other people saw him, and his desperate need to be seen as strong. Always a winner.

He loved the rallies of the faithful. He fed off the partisan crowd applause. They loved him to the point of idolatry. He had his critics, especially among the cultural elites. His appearance was mocked—the ridiculous hair, the garish fake suntan, the ties that were too long, and the suits that were too baggy. His language was criticized as limited to the range of an immature teenager. Everything was either big or beautiful: there were no shades of rhetorical sophistication. But the more the intellectual elites mocked him, the more his base supported him. Support for Trump became a signaling of populist anti-elitism. The more outrageous his tweets the more the base was persuaded that he could speak truth to power. And the obvious distaste of the elites only strengthened the support of his base. One commentator made the point that the elites took him literally but not seriously while his base took him seriously, not literally.[24]

There is a Trumpian paradox. Trump loved the unfailing support of his deep base, pandered to their fears, and embodied their anger. He gave voice to their discontent with a changing America. His emotive language and polarizing rhetoric played well with the fervent faithful, probably around 30 percent of the electorate. He bathed in their support and love. He returned to them when things got tough. But the more he pandered to this base the more he alienated middle-ground voters, centrists, and the undecided electorate. He could never hope to gain popularity with his detractors. Only days after his inauguration, a Women's Day March was organized around the world to protest his misogynistic attitudes and behaviors. In Washington, DC, the march attracted over 450,000 people. But "march" is the wrong word to describe the event—there were so many protestors that most people had to just stand in place. The small sample below of the many signs that the protestors carried shows the breadth of their animosity toward recently elected President Trump:

SuperCallousFascistRacistExtraBraggadocious

Science is real; Trump is a hoax

Ill-informed, ill-witted, illegitimate

Nyet my president

If I wanted the government in my womb, I would have
   f*&#@% a senator

Can we finally admit we've taken this "Anyone can grow
   up to be President" thing a bit too far?

Sexual assault gets 20 years in prison, not 4 years in the
   White House[25]

The hard core of anti-Trump voters constituted around
40 percent of the electorate. His core support group was predominantly White, non-college-educated males, and he steadily lost
support among college-educated women in the suburbs. That
left approximately 30 percent undecided voters (with the genuine middle probably around 15 to 20 percent). But a less than
50 percent approval rating does not translate into lack of political
power. For two years under Trump, the Republicans controlled
the presidency, the House, and the Senate, and for the entire four
years they controlled the presidency and the Senate, giving them
enough time and power to make significant changes. Among
the most significant were the gutting of the power of the various
regulatory bodies such as the Environmental Protection Agency
and the Consumer Financial Protection Board, growing restrictions on immigration, the nomination of three Supreme Court
justices, and the Tax Cuts and Jobs Act of 2017—the first major
overhaul of the tax code in thirty years—which introduced significant and permanent tax cuts in relation to corporate profits,
investment income, and estate tax. It was a boon to the wealthy.

Financial services did especially well thanks to a new lower level of corporate tax.[26]

These are significant achievements—numerous changes to codes and regulations created a more pro-business, anti-regulatory framework—but many of the regulatory changes were short-lived. Many were amended and overturned in the first year of the Biden Administration. Trump's more lasting and profound achievement was in the crystallizing of a very different America. It took three forms: the Supreme Court, the Republican Party, and a post-truth, alternative-facts United States.

First, his Supreme Court picks, confirmed by a Republican Senate, cemented the conservative bias of the Supreme Court. The nominations of three relatively young conservative jurists should ensure a right-wing court for a generation. Their lifetime nominations and the actuary tables suggest that Trump's judicial legacy could last for the next thirty years, possibly influencing the court for at least the next five presidential administrations. In future elections, the voters may choose, but an unelected Supreme Court packed with right-wing ideologues will still wield significant power over the everyday life of the Republic.

Second, although he lost suburban female voters and especially the college-educated, Trump widened the base of the Republican Party to include more extremist elements, transforming what had been a traditionally right-of-center, low-tax, pro-business, social-conservative political party into one that was more racist, xenophobic, paranoid, nationalist, and conspiracy-believing. The Republican Party had already been moving to the partisan right. Newt Gingrich promoted a scorched-earth partisanship in the 1990s. The Tea Party movement, which emerged in 2009, called for smaller government, lower deficits, and no public healthcare.

But Trump, on taking over the leadership of the party, normalized the extreme right.

The rightward shift of the Republican Party to crazyville predated Trump. There were extreme elements in the Republican Party in the 1950s, especially in the country's west. Fervent anti-communists, anti-government cells, and profoundly racist groups infected the party at local levels, especially in states like Arizona, California, and Texas. But after a purging of these elements, by around 1960, there was less difference between the two main political parties. In the South, it was the Democratic Party that was associated with White supremacy while Republicans drew on both White and Black voters for support. Starting in the 1960s, however, there was growing separation as Democrats embraced civil rights and "lost" the South. The Republican "Southern strategy" targeted and attracted White voters in the South. By the early 2000s, the two parties had very different support bases. The Republican base was whiter, more evangelical, and viewed White identity and Christian religion as under threat. Polarization was accompanied by deep feelings of anger and rage. The decline of party discipline and the rise of social media made it more difficult for the political pragmatists of either party to promote bipartisan agendas.

Political purism flourishes in times of exaggerated partisanship. Over the past thirty years there has been a rise in negative partisanship whereby Americans largely align against one party rather than affiliating with the other. Partisan media outlets, such as Fox News, reinforce this. The lack of commonalities between the two parties' supporters has made it easier for negative partisanship to flourish. As your political opponent is turned into the Un-American Other, it is easier to see your fellow citizen as an extremist and to see political pragmatism and bipartisanship not as the stuff of politics but as selling out to the enemy.

Republican John Boehner was first elected to Congress in 1991. He was part of a radical group of young congressmen, along with Newt Gingrich, who promoted a more partisan politics. Along with fellow Republicans, he voted to impeach Bill Clinton in 1998. By the time he rose to become majority leader in 2006, partisanship was so toxic that working across the aisles was seen as almost traitorous. In his memoir of his time in office, he tells of but does not name one congresswoman who informed him that if he refused her a committee assignment, she would go on Fox News to make her case. Party discipline crumbled as hyperpartisanship took over; ideologues and self-promoters were given the oxygen of publicity in the conservative media and a symbiotic relationship formed between Fox News and the right wing of the Republican Party. Boehner himself is no stranger to partisanship. He threatened to not raise the debt ceiling and to close the government down, he supported the Tea Party, and he identified with the new Republican Party radicalized by Newt Gingrich and Tea Party fundamentalism. He was radical, just not radical enough for the new Republican Party as it shifted inexorably rightward, well past traditional conservatism into conspiratorial crazydom. He resigned from Congress in 2015 when conservative opposition within his own party mounted against him.[27]

Trump inherited a Republican Party that was already moving rightwards. He just shifted it further to the fringes of the far right. He encouraged it to become more of a White nationalist, evangelical party. Conspiratorial narratives were given presidential approval, emerging from the darkness of the margins to envelop the center of Republican discourse.[28] And the crazy right it turned into was a distinctly American right. It was not the nationalist, populist right of, say, Poland, whose elected government rode to power on a platform of anti-immigration with social welfare, or the center right of the UK Conservative Party, which had to contend with a middle ground far to the left of U.S. conservatism. It was an odd blend. The new American right still contained elements of the tradition of pro-business, anti-tax, social conservatism, but with added touches of ethnonationalism and a sprinkling of xenophobia, not to mention a dash of conspiracy. It had no firm center, with changing policies toward China and Russia, a willingness to rack up deficits through generous tax cuts to the very wealthy (resulting in the third-biggest increase in annual deficit in U.S. presidential history), and an unwillingness to tackle the issue of welfare entitlements such as Social Security.[29]

Republicans were moving away from their traditional promotion of small government, hawkish foreign policy, and deregulated markets before Trump took control of the party. The shift he led was not toward a new set of policy formulations, but toward a post-political party that was not all that interested in governing.[30] The end of the Cold War had rendered the traditional anti-Soviet position obsolete, but no foreign policy narrative replaced it. Similarly, the previous promotion of small government was at odds with the stubborn popularity of government programs such as Medicare and Social Security. The rising precarity of much of the Republican base meant that even the appeal of the free-market agenda had faded. The party had to attend to the varied interests of plutocrats, populists, moralists, ethnonationalists, and racists. Republican donors still were predominantly to be found among the super-wealthy. Jason Hacker and Paul Pierson describe the dilemma of crafting an agenda that befitted the rich yet appealed to popular sentiment. The result was plutocratic populism.[31]

Trump as a politician was the embodiment of plutocratic populism; a very rich man espousing populist sentiment yet crafting specific policies that aided his business interests and donor base. The resultant political platform was an incoherent mix only held together at times by conspiratorial narratives and Trump idolatry. The growing contradictions and drift from traditional Republicanism increased as the party recentered around Trump. The Republican Party now had enough fuel and velocity to escape from the gravitational pull of mainstream America; it could orbit Trumpland, a planet where big deficits and a strangely pro-Russia stance were wrapped up in nationalist rhetoric laced with religiosity and ethnonationalism. It was an inchoate basis for an incoherent political agenda, yet it functioned to widen partisanship, ratchet up the ethnonationalist rhetoric, and narrow and solidify the party base to one of angry White men, the non-college educated, and evangelicals living in the South, in medium-sized cities, conservative suburbs, small towns, and rural areas. Trump hastened the transformation of the Republican Party from one dominated by fiscal conservatives, military hawks, and a pro-business agenda to one that eased entry to the more extreme elements on the political right.[32] The Republican Party gave a firmer foothold to a more xenophobic, white nationalist America. Trump opened up a Pandora's box of political rhetoric that previously had been on the margins and in the shadows. His presidency normalized a more extreme politics.

Trump's third biggest achievement was playing protagonist in the shift to a post-truth America. Trump's greatest political success was his cognitive capture of politics in the USA. Debates seemed to go through him, around him, be about him, and originate from him. He presided over a significant "truth decay" that heightened distrust in legitimate media, science, data, and at times even rationality. America was becoming Trumpland not in the sense that his support was growing but that his rhetoric had captured the discourse of the nation. It was both a cognitive and discursive capture as Trump shifted the national political rhetoric into a space in which truth was devalued. He turned political debates into a swamp of mendacity that poisoned the national discourse. He lied. He lied big and he lied often. He lied about the big and the small, about his enemies and sometimes even about his friends. He lied about his economic record and his achievements. He made so many baseless claims, uttered so many falsehoods that, under his presidency, America became not only a flawed democracy, but a post-truth state.

His presidency started with a small lie about the crowd on the mall in 2017 and ended with the Big Lie that fueled the insurrection. In the speech at the Ellipse on January 6, 2021, Trump made more than one hundred false claims about the election. The claims should come as no surprise from even a cursory understanding of Donald Trump. His fragile ego could not countenance losing. It had to have been stolen. What is unsurprising, then, is not that he claimed the election had been stolen from him, but that his claims were believed by so many. In the following chapters I will try to explore the structural reasons why the Big Lie was so widely believed.

2

Losing Trust in Government

On January 6, 2021, in Washington, DC, between 10,000 and 20,000 people gathered to protest the congressional confirmation of Joe Biden as the next president of the United States. The crowd faced the incumbent president, Donald Trump, who told them that the recent election was stolen and that he was the rightful winner. He stoked their anger, fluffed their rage, and directed them to walk to the Capitol, where hundreds then broke into the building and disrupted proceedings in order to overturn the results of a legitimate election. There are many reasons for the event. In this chapter, we will look at one important factor, the loss of trust in government. Let's begin with the unlikely pairing of Obama and Trump.

Obama, Trump, and the U.S. Legitimation Crisis

Trump and Obama have a complex history. While Barack Obama was president, from 2009 to 2016, Donald Trump—arguably more than anyone else at the time—helped to spread the lie that Obama was not born in the United States. It was a clear attempt at undermining and delegitimizing the first Black U.S. president. The "birther" controversy, as it became known, was fervently fueled by Trump and silently endorsed by a Republican Party that failed to offer any resistance to Trump's lies. The lies were too useful. For the official Republican Party, Trump's birther tweets helped to keep the base motivated, undermine Obama, and weaken the Democrats' political agenda. The brazen claim that the president was not a citizen and was thus an illegal president fed into the conspiratorial narratives that were gaining strength and widely diffusing across new media platforms. The birther conspiracy had many authors, but Trump, with his large social media following, kindled it into mainstream Republican rhetoric. Trump thrust Obama into a broader conspiracy centered around anti-u.s. forces and shadowy foreigners at work. Thus, so the logic goes, Obama was not just a political rival, but a danger to the Republic. And in a taste of things to come, no senior Republican figure came forward with a strong denial of Trump's claims. The Republican establishment thought it could cynically use Trump to its advantage, mobilizing the grassroots and galvanizing the donor base. This was the start of a descent into not only condoning but actively encouraging a conspiratorial narrative. The social scientist Dan Ariely makes the point that dishonesty arises not from a lack of character but from an abundance of opportunity. Trump and his "birther" lie presented an occasion for the Republicans to undermine their political rival at no real cost to themselves. Ariely goes on to point out that big deceptions arise gradually from small lies. Each minor, though "convenient," deception can lead to more and increasingly larger deceptions, incrementally small perhaps but over the course of time leading to fundamentally compromised positions. Like going downstairs into a dark cave, one step at a time, the Republicans gradually lost sight of the light of truth in their journey from the birther lie to the Big Lie and into the growing darkness.[1]

Obama initially resisted the demand to release his birth certificate. Yet he eventually did so in 2011 when he included the controversy as part of his speech at the annual White House Correspondents' Dinner. Having evolved into a major annual social event, the dinner is attended by celebrities invited by the media companies to give their tables some glamour, luster, and pizzazz. A jarring and unlikely mixture of Washington insiders and movie stars, the Hollywood equivalent would be if the speaker of the House and the head of the congressional Budget Office were invited to the Academy Awards. By 2011, the Correspondents' Dinner had become an important event in Washington's social–political calendar—an inside-the-Beltway equivalent of a Hollywood Oscar party—and Trump was invited to sit at the *Washington Post* table. The *Post* considered his celebrity status more important than his birther lies. His popularity trumped his dangerous rhetoric. The prevalent sense of the gathering was that Trump was a bit of a joke, colorful, and brash, capable of generating media interest but not a serious political figure. The consensus was his birther lies were not a reason not to invite him to the dinner. He generated enough hype to dispel any misgivings from the leading newspaper in the city and one of the most influential in the entire country. The audience listened to the president and an invited comedian, Seth Meyers. Obama mentioned the release of his birth certificate and went on to mock Trump in a deadpan style:

> Now, I know that he's taken some flak lately, but no one is happier, no one is prouder to put this birth certificate matter to rest than The Donald. And that's because he can finally get back to focusing on the issues that matter—like,

did we fake the moon landing? What really happened in Roswell? And where are Biggie and Tupac?[2]

Meyers followed Obama and poked even more fun at Trump, who sat unsmiling throughout the entire routine. Trump was publicly humiliated by Obama's clever remarks and Meyers's more direct attacks.

The event has multiple interpretations. An article in the *New Yorker* saw it as a pivotal moment, perhaps even priming Trump's long-held presidential ambitions. But another journalist, from the *Washington Post*, also present at the dinner, saw little significance. The dinner became a sort of "Rashomon" event, a moment recalled differently by contrary witnesses. I recall watching the dinner live on television and remember Trump's extreme discomfort with Obama's remarks and his smoldering rage at Meyers. Whether it led to or confirmed his decision to run in 2016 is another matter.[3]

Trump and Obama. Their sequential occupation of the White House made the contrasting comparisons between them that much easier to make. One White, the other Black; one, a product of privilege and entitlement; the other, an embodiment of a more meritocratic arc. Trump gave wooden speeches and seemed incapable of empathy or self-deprecation, and his ideas were expressed in inarticulate sentences that only came to life when filled with rage and resentment. Obama was a superb orator, capable of emotional connections. He could laugh at himself. He was very often a better stand-up at the Correspondents' Dinner than the professional comedians hired specifically for the event. Obama was articulate and seemed a natural public speaker, entirely at ease. One seemed comfortable in his own skin; the other had a bottomless ego that required, and indeed demanded, public acts of fealty.

The Trump–Obama nexus continued even as Obama retired from the presidency, after serving the maximum of two terms, sliding into the strange afterlife of a living ex-president, signing a book deal, keeping out of politics, making money, and working on charitable endeavors. As president, Trump's policy objectives would vary and veer, yet one constant theme was the need to overturn anything that had been proposed by Obama, and then go one better than Obama's accomplishments. The unilateral cancellation of the treaty with Iran, the withdrawal from the Paris Agreement on climate change, and repeated attempts to overturn the Affordable Care Act (Obamacare, Obama's signal domestic policy achievement) were all part of a calculated plan by Trump to surpass or diminish Obama's achievements. At times it appeared that Trump's only motivating force was his anti-Obama agenda. Trump's attempted rapprochement with North Korea's leader was in large measure part of a conscious attempt to win the Nobel Prize, a notable—if questionable—Obama achievement.

They were so very different. Obama had a meritocratic rise and embodied a post-racial American Dream. Trump, on the other hand, was the American Reality of inherited wealth and White privilege. Born into a fortune, his life has always been cushioned and carpeted. Obama is intellectually curious and was sometimes emotionally cool as president but capable of empathy when the occasion demanded. Trump seems neither intellectually curious nor capable of empathy.

Yet it would be a mistake to focus too much on their differences because they both represented discontent with the existing order. Despite the vast differences, we should also consider what shared experiences connect them. Both were, of course, elected president of a country going through difficult times: the postimperial reordering of foreign affairs, the lingering effects of an economy slowly leaving a recession, massive socioeconomic changes, and a reduced leadership role in the world. There was also the similarly insurgent nature of their presidencies. Obama was a young, idealistic Illinois state senator when he ran for the u.s. Senate in 2004. He won in a landslide. He was the u.s. senator for Illinois for little more than three years when he ran for the nomination for the Democratic candidate for president. He won the nomination and went on to defeat John McCain in a historic presidential election. He was the first Black man to be elected to the presidency, and the result was not close. For many liberals it seemed like the beginning of post-racial America, the stain of slavery almost washed away by Obama's stunning victory: he won 52.9 percent of the popular vote and 365 Electoral College votes to McCain's 173. Obama won big in the northeast, the far west, and upper Midwest. The South was solidly Republican. McCain's recruitment of Sarah Palin as his running mate was a short-term fix for a flagging campaign, but one, as it turned out, with longer-term consequences for the Republican Party as a new aggressive populism was added to their platform.

Obama's victories in the Democratic nomination and in the first presidential election were against much more traditional party candidates. In the primary he defeated the Democratic insider Hillary Clinton, and in the general election he bested Republican stalwart John McCain. Both were seasoned politicians with decades of experience and a dense circuitry of party connections. Obama, in contrast, was a young Black man with few legislative accomplishments and without a long record to run on, but he had cast one significant vote: as a u.s. senator in 2007 he voted against supplying more defense funds to prolong the occupation of Iraq.

As an Illinois senator in 2002 he publicly opposed the invasion of Iraq. He was the nearest thing to an insurgent candidate, someone who didn't go along with the party hacks, Democrats as well as Republicans, who supported the catastrophic invasion of Iraq. His critical stance was prescient given the subsequent fiasco of failed strategy and mindless tactics that eventually turned the American people against the war. He was different. Something new. Some of the shine rubbed off after his first administration, as it always does. He lost some support in his presidential campaign of 2012 but still won 51 percent of the popular vote and 332 electoral votes to Mitt Romney's 206. The only state Obama lost in 2012 compared to 2008 was Indiana, a foretaste of more Democratic losses to come in the 2016 election in the upper Midwest.

Obama defeated establishment figures. He mobilized support among minorities and young people, and he expanded the Democratic base by persuading those in the middle that he was neither a scary proposition nor a traditional candidate. His lack of experience was considered an advantage by an electorate looking for someone beyond the traditional political norm. While perhaps not as radical as some of his more liberal supporters would have liked, the promise of Obama was of something new, something different, a welcome change.

★★★

Trump was a similarly insurgent political figure: he was not part of the traditional political establishment. He was from the world of real estate deals, TV reality shows, beauty pageants, and social media. He was not a traditional Republican candidate any more than he was a genuine populist. He also had a complicated personal life: married three times, divorced twice, a vigorous dating history, and persistent rumors of extramarital affairs and cases of sexual harassment. Not the standard résumé of a presidential candidate. He was boastful of his wealth and prided himself on being one of the "1 percent." Like Obama, he was not from the usual political world, and this made him even more able—it seemed to many people—to step into Washington and break up the established order. He was elected not to protect or sustain the establishment order but to destroy it. Trump's appeal to the deep-state conspiracy believers, such as QAnon, is only understandable if we realize that many saw him from the outset as a destroyer of a corrupt system. QAnon, as we will see later, just took the narrative to a more bizarre level.

Obama's stunning victory in the presidential election of 2008 was equally as disruptive as Trump's remarkable victory in 2016. Obama was not a stranger to the halls of Congress, but as a one-term senator barely out of Illinois politics he was not a seasoned Washington insider. Trump was proud of his outsider status and touted his lack of political experience as an advantage. It was a connection to the people who felt left out of inside-the-Beltway politics. Both men won astounding, surprising, and norm-breaking elections. Neither achieved all of his goals, but both shared a defining characteristic: they were elected as a reaction to and disrupters of the status quo. Obama's failure was his inability to fully challenge the status quo; Trump's failing was his attempted destruction of it.

★ ★ ★

Obama's support came more from the younger generation, minorities, and the college-educated, while Trump relied more on the older generation, White males, evangelicals, and blue-collar types.

People voted in support of Obama or Trump for many different reasons, but they shared the same sense that something was deeply wrong with their country. Obama and Trump were elected because of the same underlying legitimation crisis sweeping the United States.

The German philosopher and sociologist Jürgen Habermas outlined several potential crises in democratic capitalist societies: a *fiscal crisis* is when expenditure is more than revenue, an *economic crisis* occurs when the economy fails to meet popular expectations, a *rationality crisis* is the failure to make the correct decisions, and a *legitimation crisis* can be defined as loss of popular support for the institution of government, not just the office holders. The United States may be in the difficult position of experiencing all of these at the same time. Trust and confidence in government waxes and wanes: an unpopular war or economic recession deflates the numbers, only to be reinflated when the war ends or when the economy picks up again. But the ending of the long postwar boom along with declining confidence in the economic globalization project pursued by the political and business elites has raised a structural rather than just a temporal crisis of confidence.[4]

In a poll conducted in January 2012 by Rasmussen Reports, 60 percent of people interviewed in a telephone survey responded that they felt the country was going in the wrong direction. Eight years later, in September 2020, it was 69 percent. Other surveys reveal similarly high levels of disapproval. The decline is even more marked over a longer term. The Pew Research Center has conducted polls on how much u.s. citizens trust the federal government. In 1964 more than 70 percent of respondents recorded trust in the institution. By November 2015 that number had fallen to 19 percent, less than one in five Americans. A Gallup

Poll survey revealed only 20 percent of those polled had trust in the presidency and only 6 percent had trust in Congress.[5]

There is a darkening mood to the national spirit. Not only is there a lack of confidence in specific government policies, but also belief in the idea of government itself is at an all-time low. Across the spectrum of political opinion, there is a profound sense that the country has lost its way. Compounding the feeling of malaise, there is no general agreement as to which direction it should be headed. Election results do not seem to solve the deadlock, only enhance it. The United States remains a house divided. While some propose even more military spending, deeper tax cuts, and further deregulation, others argue that this is exactly the policy that got us into the present mess. While the sense of pessimism and the feeling that the country is floundering are shared among citizens, there is no general agreement on the way forward. I suggest that there are six major reasons for this current legitimation crisis: the growing hold of the narrative that government is the problem, the hollowing out of the middle class and the ending of the American Dream, increasing polarization, stark generational differences, the enthronement of financial capitalism, and the regressive effects of globalization. Let's look at each in turn.

Government Is the Problem

At his inauguration address, on January 20, 1981, Ronald Reagan said, "Government is not the solution to our problem; government is the problem."[6] A strange thing to say for someone who had fought so vigorously for the government's top job. But let's pass over the obvious inconsistencies in the argument, because Reagan's remark constitutes an important strain of political thought in the United States. Distrust of government is common in many countries across the world. But in the States it is baked into the prevailing political attitudes, embodied in populist ideology, reinforced by one of the only two main political parties, and in recent decades espoused by economic elites in the promotion of neoliberalism, an ideology shaped by a constellation of political interests and constituencies that promotes deregulation, limited government, and unwavering support for the market system.

Distrust in governmental power was a foundational feature of the Republic. Whereas modern political constitutions seek to expand the reach of government power, the u.s. Constitution was devised to highlight its limits. It was organized as a separation of powers not only between individual states and the federal government but between Congress, the Supreme Court, and the presidency. The founders of the Republic were very wary of concentrated political power. Their political ideology was dominated by the desire to safeguard individual rights from the press of governmental authority. Thomas Jefferson, for example, was keen to draw a wall of separation between Church and State. Not simply for fear of the state intervening in religious affairs and religious freedoms but because religious affairs can too easily and too often influence government and impact individual political freedoms.

In the federal system of government there was always complex interaction between the federal government and the states. States' rights and federal power are often locked in conflict. The American Civil War was the bloodiest of them all, a rupture sprung from slavery and the right to secede. Today, issues such as civil rights, abortion, or mask mandates continue to pit states' rights against federal supremacy. Other ideas and movements were grafted onto this general wariness of government, influenced frequently by the blowback of the rich. Whenever political power shifted, so that government was more involved in the redistribution of wealth, the oligarchy attacked the very right of government to intervene. Many in the economic elite railed against Roosevelt's New Deal as an unwarranted expression of government power against their wealth and influence.[7] The rich, then as now, tend to worry about government when government becomes more involved in redistributing wealth.

The Republican Party has relied on the distrust of governments to great effect. In the 1950s, Senator Joe McCarthy raised questions about the loyalty of u.s. government officials. His smear campaign helped to give oxygen to the notion that government could not be trusted. In the 1960s Republicans employed a "Southern strategy" to woo White southerners away from the Democratic Party. They appealed to the notion of states' power to contest federal government direction on civil rights. Their campaign was spectacularly successful as the South moved from heavily Democratic to reliably Republican. Republican Party strategists realized that criticizing central government could be a vote winner.

There was also a distrust of government among left-leaning voters. Criticisms centered on the abuse of government power and the notion of a corporate industrial state with a too-cozy relationship between major businesses and government. A staple of leftist ideology was that the government was in the pocket of big business. The combined result of Republican vote pandering and Democratic criticism was a spectacular drop in trust in government from 77 percent in October 1964 to 36 percent in December 1974.[8]

In the 1990s the same political discourse was again employed, this time by a Republican Party led by Newt Gingrich. In the battle to gain control over Congress, Gingrich inaugurated a more aggressive attack on Democrats. Political talk can be abrasive and, in fact, *should be* in a functioning democracy. Yet Gingrich took the rhetoric to a new level, one in which political opponents were deemed so untrustworthy that if they were in control of government, government could not be trusted. The rhetoric became part of the Republican DNA used to mobilize their base, activate their donors, and attract independent voters. In this more partisan context, it was a small step from an untrustworthy government to the notion of the deep state, a secret cabal inside government following its own evil agenda rather than the will of the people. Trump's own use of the term "deep state" built on decades of Republican rhetoric that worked to sow doubt about government itself. From Reagan's inaugural remark to Trump's evocation of the deep state, the American political public was fed a constant narrative about the untrustworthiness of government.[9]

Even when government works to provide goods and benefits, they are often hidden in private delivery systems. The political scientist Suzanne Mettler describes how subsidies and benefits given to the middle class are concealed and submerged. Tax relief on mortgage interest payments, retirement benefits, and private health plans, for example, are not seen as government subsidies at all. The positive role of government is not given credit and the subsidized benefits to middle- and upper-class recipients are hidden from public scrutiny.[10]

The anti-government political rhetoric was not just a populist expression. It was used by elites who argued for the adoption of neoliberalism. This ideology started as a response to the New

Deal–Keynesian movement, named after its public policy expression in the United States and its prime economic theorist, John Maynard Keynes (1883–1946), who argued for the benefits of government spending to ward off economic depression and recession. From 1933 to the mid-1970s Keynesian economics was a dominant economic ideology that held great appeal in societies with popular left-wing parties and strong organized labor. It relied on a deep and wide tax base, a commitment to the redistribution of wealth through progressive taxation, and a belief that government could fine-tune the economy and solve many social problems. Government was a solution to the social and economic ills of society. It was always weaker in the United States, where ideas of individual rights often trumped collective goals. The Democratic Party until the 1970s was lukewarm in its pursuit of universal welfare coverage because of its strong racist voter base in the South. The u.s. labor movement was concerned more with promoting the interests of its members than with promoting social justice for all citizens.

As elements of the welfare state became embodied in government policies and tax regimes, the United States saw the rise of an alternative economic ideology, neoliberalism, which emerged from the works of such thinkers as Friedrich Hayek (1899–1992), who baulked at the post-Second World War Keynesian welfare state. Neoliberal ideology was popularized for political consumption by right-wing think tanks and, from the 1980s onwards, diffused across the West to achieve economic orthodoxy and political dominance. It bent the discourse so that even oppositional politics were impacted by its abiding presence. It shaped u.s. political and economic opinion for decades and across different administrations. The main ideas centered on reducing the size and influence of the state, promoting deregulation, and encouraging unfettered market forces. Promoted by Reagan and successive Republican presidents, it was solidified by Bill Clinton and unchallenged by Obama.[11]

Neoliberalism gained traction in the United States because the commitment to New Deal Keynesian policies was more luke-warm than in Western Europe and especially in contrast to the Nordic democracies. It was thus more vulnerable to the neo-liberalist counterargument. Milton Friedman (1912–2006), a Nobel Prize-winning economist, lauded the virtues of free markets and small, limited governments. His bestselling book *Free to Choose*, published in 1980, linked individual freedoms with functioning markets and restrained governments. Unregulated markets were the solution, and government was the problem. This agenda's core proposition is that deregulated markets will increase economic growth and raise living standards. Government had to be shrunk and neutered. Neoliberalism's greatest success was in the financial sector. The most profound economic and political change in the last thirty years was the decline of the New Deal USA, which regulated banks and provided social welfare, and the rise of Wall Street USA. From the 1980s to the 1990s, we witnessed the accelerating financialization of society. The financial sector is now bigger, richer, and more powerful than ever before and, in a disturbing trend, as its interests diverge from those of Main Street or the real economy, its hold over the political system increases. Both Democrats and Republicans worked to undercut the regulations in place since the New Deal that limited the power of finance. And as the shackles were loosened, the concentration of power continued and even more money flowed from the bankers to the politicians. There was a revolving door between Wall Street and the political establishment. It was a totally non-partisan affair as Hank Paulson, Robert Rubin, Timothy Geithner, and Larry Summers moved from key government posts to lucrative gigs with banks and hedge funds, before sometimes moving back into politics again. And in an act that sealed the alliance, the political establishment bailed out the banks in 2008. Later, in an act of political deafness, or perhaps as a result of donor demand, the Obama Administration appointed Geithner, directly involved in the deal, to become Treasury secretary. The 2008/9 bailout of a corrupt financial system signaled the full extent of Wall Street's hijacking of government.[12]

The shift from a highly regulated banking and finance sector to a much more deregulated one reinforced the rise of finance capitalism to a position of dominance. Banks and financial institutions not only got bigger in the lead-up to the 2008 financial crash, they achieved cognitive capture. Their interests are seen as tantamount to the national interest. Deregulation allowed the sector to grow and expand, and this expansion created a powerful force to keep pushing for more deregulation. During the expansion, checks and balances were withdrawn, overturned, or ignored. Financial institutions were allowed to take on greater amounts of risk because returns were higher. Prudence and probity became old-fashioned concepts in a world of high returns and bloated compensation packages. And when things went bad, really bad, the government was used to bail out the banking system. The bailout of the banking system in the late 2000s led in turn to the rise of the Tea Party Movement and even more distrust in government. As households lost their homes and neighborhoods were devastated by the rising foreclosure rate, the official response was to give money to the banks with few, if any, regulations. It was clear to most of the general public that the powerful financial institutions had captured the federal government. Public discontent, exemplified by the rise of the Tea Party, soon hardened to a cynicism about Wall Street owning the political parties. This distrust is baked into the present legitimation crisis, with many Americans convinced that the country is controlled by a cabal of rich bankers, hedge fund managers, and venture capitalists.

Over the last three decades, powerful economic and political trends have reinforced the notion that government is the problem: it hinders economic growth, infringes on individual rights, and, when administered by political opponents, is a source of chaos and national weakening. These ideas are central to today's Republican Party. With Trump at the helm, it became a very small and easy step to take from seeing government as a problem to believing the paranoid idea of a shadowy deep state working against the interests of hardworking Americans.

A Hollowed-out Middle and the End of the American Dream

Distrust in government was reinforced by the basic failure of the U.S. government to protect the living standards of the population. The government presided over a decline in middle-class living standards amidst growing inequality. The rich got richer, as the middle class was squeezed.

Over the past forty years, the White, non-college-educated population has experienced a decline in numerical significance, an erosion of living standards, and a perceived marginalization in terms of the broader culture of the country. In many rural areas and small towns and in former industrial areas of the U.S.

economy, many jobs have been lost and few good jobs have been created to replace them. The changing nature of American society, the hollowing out of the middle class, and the growing precarity of many has shaken belief in the American Dream, especially for the non-college educated, many of whom feel that the dream has been lost or at worst stolen from them.

The undermining of the u.s. middle class began in the 1970s and has accelerated since 2000. Many factors are at work, but one of the most talked about is "deindustrialization." Manufacturing jobs have long provided entrance into a more economically secure middle class for non-college-educated workers. These types of jobs have declined dramatically. There were 18 million manufacturing jobs in the usa in 1984. By 2018, it was a little under 12 million. This was a dramatic reduction in well-paying jobs.[13] There are many reasons behind this decline, including technological progress reducing the need for human labor as well as trade policies that made it easier for foreign manufacturers to offload their cheaper goods. There was also a global shift in manufacturing from the developed world to the developing world because of lower production costs, including wages, in the latter regions and cheapening transport. While a new middle class was being created in Japan, South Korea and China, the blue-collar middle class was eroded in the usa. Many feel a sense of political betrayal. In the United States, popular sentiments are often not given political articulation by the two mainstream parties. The Republican Party used its post-Reagan, working-class base as electoral cannon fodder to promote an agenda that aided its big donors. The blue-collar base was fed rhetoric while the business wing received all the benefits of free trade and a weakening of organized labor. The rhetoric was effective in undermining the legitimacy of not only Democratic administrations, but government itself. Trump is only the most recent embodiment of this, but it began earlier with Reagan's assertion that government itself was the problem. Meanwhile, the Democratic administrations of Clinton and Obama pursued an economic agenda that promoted globalization.

If the Republicans had a trickle-down theory that maintained, despite evidence to the contrary, that making the rich richer would benefit everyone, the Democratic equivalent was that the benefits of globalization would eventually raise all boats. Maybe, in the long term. But in the short to medium term, where we live, it negatively impacted the bottom 50 percent. Many of the blue-collar workers felt ignored by Democrats who promoted economic globalization that undercut their jobs and a cultural relativism that undermined their values. Cynically used by the Republicans and shabbily treated by the Democrats, many turned to Trump. As a family-made millionaire, he was not an obvious standard-bearer of the marginalized, but his outsider status and maverick campaign resonated with a substantial mass of Americans who harbored a sense of alienation from the mainstream political parties. Trump was only the most recent embodiment of this Republican anti-government platform. He added the conspiratorial twist of the deep state.

One of the biggest impacts of recent changes in the American economy has been the bifurcation between the college educated and non-college educated. People who have at least a bachelor's degree constitute around 35 percent of the 2020 population. The remaining two-thirds of the population, those without a college degree, make less money, die younger, and have poorer health outcomes. A new class divide has emerged that separates those with and those without a college degree. The latter are more likely to be divorced, suffer from depression and drug abuse, and have more debilitating illnesses. They are 40 percent more likely to be unemployed and four times more likely to be living in poverty. And the differences between the two groups have only widened in the last thirty years as those without a college degree in America lead more stressful lives. Anne Case and Angus Deaton provide a detailed and depressing story of the increasing divide between college- and non-college-educated Americans. From 1980 to 2020, real wages declined for non-college-educated men aged 25–54. There was also a widening gap in health and mortality. Let's take just one statistic. Between 1990 and 2018, death rates for college-educated White non-Hispanics aged between 50 and 54 remained under 50 per 100,000. For the similar non-college-educated group, that figure rose to almost 200. In other words, the mortality rate for non-college-educated Americans increased fourfold. The greatest percentage increase was for White women without a college degree, especially for those living in small towns and rural areas where many women had to bear the load of holding families together at a time of unemployment and opioid addiction. The takeaway from the detailed work of Case and Deaton is that there is a growing class divide in wages, living standards, and health outcomes between those with and those without a college degree. They documented the unraveling of the lives of many in this non-college-educated group as restricted employment opportunities and declining living standards combine to produce a loss of meaning, exclusion from what's perceived as a good life, and diminished status. Across a range of measures, from rates of unhappiness to incidence of chronic pain, heavy drinking, church attendance, and divorce rates, there are large and widening differences between college-educated and non-college-educated Americans. Those without a degree have seen their wages and life expectancies decline and their mortality rates increase.[14]

A college degree in itself does not guarantee mobility. Analysis by the Economic Policy Institute showed how the average wage premium for college-educated workers barely changed from 2000 to 2020. Most of the economic gains were taken by the very rich and by only a small proportion of college graduates. Wages for the bottom 60 percent of college graduates are lower today than they were in 2000.[15] The pursuit of a college degree can be an expensive burden, with 40 percent of student loan borrowers unable to complete their degree.[16]

Other societies experienced similar trends of deindustrialization, the decline of blue-collar jobs, and widening inequality. However, most had stronger social safety nets, with higher welfare benefits and better public health programs that softened the downward spiral. These benefits came at a cost, of course, with higher taxation levels than in the United States. But in the United States, the benefits of lower taxation accrue to the higher-income groups while the lack of a safety net exposes the lower-income groups to a harder life. The political philosopher Isaiah Berlin once made a distinction between two types of liberty: negative liberty is a sort of bubble that protects the individual from the state, the right to be left alone; positive liberty, on the other hand, is the right to be cared for.[17] Negative liberty abounds in the United States but positive liberty is lacking for the less well-off. The differences between the two forms are less noticeable when economies are booming and incomes are rising, as in the 1950s and '60s, but they become marked during economic transformations such as the one that hollowed out the U.S.

middle class. The result is that positive liberty is enjoyed by the wealthier while the lack of political liberty is borne most heavily by the poor.

These economic and cultural changes are experienced in different ways. Arlie Russell Hochschild's fieldwork took her into one of the poorest areas of the United States, the Louisiana Bayou Country, which has one of the lowest life expectancies and poorest health outcomes in the nation, due in part to the environmental crisis brought on by the pollution from factories of major chemical companies. These conditions have not led to a renewed class-consciousness or a sense among the bayou residents that capitalism has failed them. The conditions did not provoke an outburst of anti-capitalism. Socialism has made few inroads into either mainstream America or its economically humbler fringes. Rather, most people in this Louisiana region see their poor living conditions, their cultural marginalization, and their relative economic decline as the result of a federal government run by coastal elites. In their eyes, the system is biased against them, and others (read, immigrants and non-whites) are able to jump the queue in pursuit of the American Dream. Donald Trump connected with them not through calls to their economic self-interest but by voicing their anger and resentment at the "establishment" and "others." He appealed to their sense of victimhood. In 2012, across the country, White non-college-educated voters polled almost equally for Democrats and Republicans.[18] By 2016, Trump had a 39-point margin in this group compared to Hillary Clinton.[19]

There has been a shift in the relative power and bargaining strength of capital compared to labor. Capital can move easily and quickly around the globe in search of cheaper labor and lower production costs. Labor, in contrast, is stuck in place.

The decline of organized labor, with only one in ten workers in a union, versus one in three in the 1950s, further weakened labor's bargaining power, and the net result was a shift in wealth and political influence from labor to capital and from the middle class to the rich.[20] The changes now extend into the white-collar sector as companies pursue productivity and profits while also cutting benefits. In the past fifty years, the bedrock of the nation's institutional democracy, the American middle class, has been squeezed and battered. The income of non-college-educated males has been static, while household costs have increased, meaning more members of the household have had to seek employment. Other countries in the global North, including much of Western Europe, experienced similar effects of the global shift in manufacturing and a weakening of labor. However, the social wage, by which I mean the basket of goods and benefits that citizens in the richer social democracies receive, is so much smaller in the United States. Universal healthcare, for example, is a public good in much of Europe, the same with pre-K education. Workers across Western Europe get more holi-days and more social benefits than their American counterparts. Taxation is higher in those European countries, but, as men-tioned, the smaller tax burdens in the United States constitute a greater benefit to the wealthiest. In the States, there is no man-dated paid family leave and pre-K education is expensive. Many women, in particular, have to shoulder a double burden of work-ing both outside and inside the home. Today, the United States can be a harsh country to live in for working households.

Many Republican-controlled states hardened the punitive nature of social welfare through low unemployment benefits and administrative systems more designed to prevent people from accessing welfare than help those in distress. In the USA, many people are only one or two missed paychecks away from losing decent health coverage and, in some cases, facing financial collapse. Between 1979 and 2015, while the three middle quintiles of income distribution saw their family income rise 46 percent, the top quintile saw an increase of 103 percent. Not only was there a decline in wages, but there was also less upward mobility. In the past forty years the United States has experienced stagnating wages, declining mobility, and growing inequality as most of the benefits of economic growth go to the top 1 percent. The inequality is not only increasing but becoming more entrenched as children are often less likely to achieve the living standards of their parents. The real question is not why there is a legitimation crisis, but why—in the light of all these changes—it has taken so long to crystallize.[21]

Increasing Polarization

The rightward shift of the Republican Party is linked to the increasing polarization in U.S. politics. Political partisanship has long been part of everyday politics in the States. However, it has been growing in recent years alongside other changes in the country. Previously marginalized groups such as Black people, LGBTQ+, and women now demand a larger role in the political discourse. There are more foreign immigrants. The possibility of a secure middle-class life for those without a college degree is fast disappearing. All these characteristics challenge traditional notions of what America should sound like, look like and be. While some people feel heartened by the progressive moves, others are deeply disturbed. There is a toxic mix of cultural anxiety, economic pain, and political anger. Politics is becoming less about the mundane and managerial concerns such as deciding about the proper rate of income tax, and more about the very soul of the nation. The polarization is reinforced by the splintering of media options that allow readers, viewers, and listeners to have their opinions and beliefs reinforced and amplified rather than debated or challenged. In the closed circuitry of partisan media, the differences are amped up to rancorous levels.

There is also a link between growing income inequality and increasing political polarization. As incomes demonstrably widen and social mobility is limited, political anger becomes more prominent. Feeling poor in relation to others, especially with declining opportunity to improve your position—or even worse, a perception that your way forward is blocked—results in all kinds of social and political consequences, from declining health outcomes to reduced life expectancy and being more vulnerable to political polarization and the lure of conspiracy theories.[22]

There is an asymmetric polarization. The Republican Party has shifted not just toward the right, but to the fringes of the far right. The Republican Party has since the 1990s become a more extremist force ripping apart the big tent of moderate bipartisanship. And it's only getting worse. Two respected commentators wrote a book published in 2012 with the title *It's Even Worse Than It Looks* that pointed to the role of the Republican Party in creating intolerant politics and governing paralysis. The 2015 edition, which again highlighted the broken, dysfunctionally partisan political system, had a slightly different title, *It's Even Worse Than It Was*.[23]

Part of the polarization reflects racial differences. In the 1950s South, the Democratic Party was associated with White supremacy while Republicans appealed to all voters. Starting in the 1960s, however, there was growing separation as Democrats embraced civil rights and effectively "lost" the White voters of the South. The Republicans saw an opportunity. They used their "Southern strategy" to attract White voters in the South.[24] By the early 2000s, the two parties had different support bases. The Republicans had become whiter and more evangelical. Many hardcore Trump supporters saw White identity and their religion as under threat. The polarization was not just in support of the parties, it was an affective polarization, now embellished and adorned with deep feelings of anger and rage. So, while one-third of the United States thought Trump was great for the country, another third saw him as a mortal threat to the Republic.

Political anger and partisanship are also caused and reinforced by the mismatch between voters and policy outcomes. Most Americans, for example, want some form of gun control, but it has been impossible to achieve this at the federal level.[25] Powerful alliances, and individuals influenced by industry interests, operate to frustrate the will of the people. When they do so, anger is stoked, and citizens become even more partisan.

The very nature of government in the United States is also an important factor. Winning an election does not guarantee the ability to enact policy. The divided and fragmented government as we have it today has contrived to make the link between winning an election and enacting legislation tenuous at best. So, the party that wins tends to have a hard time governing, while the party not in power has no incentive to help in governing. The result is an intensification of polarizing, vitriolic rhetoric. The arguments intensify, while few policies are enacted. The decline of party discipline and the rise of social media have also made it more difficult for political pragmatists of either party to promote bipartisan agendas. Political purism flourishes and reinforces partisanship. The past forty years have seen a rise in negative partisanship whereby Americans largely align against one party rather than affiliating with the other. Partisan media outlets reinforce this negative partisanship, which has flourished because of the lack of commonalities between the two parties' supporters. As your political opponent is turned into the Un-American Other, it is easier to see them as not fellow citizens but extremists and to see political pragmatism and bipartisanship not as the very stuff of politics but as selling out to the enemy.

Generational Differences

There are lucky and unlucky generations. Those born in good times get advantages over those born in bad times. If you were born in the United States in the period 1935 to 1955 you were carried along on the great postwar expansion of economic growth, rising incomes, and new and extended benefits. If you were White, it was easy to get a job, obtain a federally subsidized mortgage, and do well. People could leave school and get a good job earning the equivalent of $16 an hour. The United States ended the Second World War in much better shape than its prewar economic rivals and that advantage lasted for almost twenty years before the rest of the world caught up and could compete directly with the Americans in the global marketplace. By the early 1970s, the u.s. competitive advantage that undergirded the creation of a large and affluent middle class was coming to an end. The long postwar boom in the United States, which helped to create a White middle class who thought that it was their own hard work and American birthright, not historical contingency, that led to their affluence, was disappearing into recurring economic crisis against a backdrop of increasing inequality.

The boom had coincided with a marked downturn in the number and presence of foreign-born people living in the United States, the proportion of whom fell dramatically from almost 15 percent in 1910 to 4.7 percent in 1970. The Great Depression led to a period of stricter immigration control that lasted from around 1930 until 1970. The number of immigrants coming to the United States during those decades fell off sharply. In other words, growing up in the postwar United States, you experienced a period of economic growth with a declining number of foreign-born citizens and fewer immigrant arrivals. While the country was getting richer, there was a marked decrease in immigrant and first-generation Americans. Then just as the long boom started to dip, the numbers of immigrants increased. By 2015, according to the u.s. Census, the proportion of foreign-born Americans reached 13.4 percent. There were 43 million immigrants, unevenly distributed to be sure, but numerous enough in many places to constitute a political force at the local, state, and national levels. More multiple identities such as African American, Asian American, and Cuban American also became more more commonly used as as population descriptors and mobilized as political groups.

There were other changes that accelerated after 1979. More women entered the workforce, resulting in the nuclear family— mom, dad, and two kids—becoming a minority family unit, compared to the rise in the number and proportion of single-person households and households without children. The LGBTQ+ and Black communities mobilized to overcome generations of discrimination. It was a changing world, and for many of those brought up in a country dominated by a White, nativist, traditional family-structured society, this new America was a threat to their traditional values. For many, their mounting economic difficulties and the social and cultural changes created a sense of alienation and marginalization. One study found that support for Trump in 2016 was less about financial well-being and more about fears of globalization and the rise of a majority–minority America.[26] Trump was drawing less on economic insecurity and more on status threats, especially to Whites, Christians, and men. He mainly appealed to those experiencing anxiety derived from a perceived loss of status.

If you were born after 1985, in contrast, you were born into a more multicultural society, where rights had been extended beyond the traditional White masculine core. Women, LGBTQ+, and racial minorities were more visible and more audible. The generational difference partitioned America into a more diverse, economically uncertain country. If you were born in 1990, you entered the job market during the Great Recession, amid the prospect of a generation of stagnant incomes and increasing costs. Generational inequity kicks in when those paying for the support of the elderly are, for a variety of reasons (including the relative decline in wages and incomes), unlikely to see the same benefits. Older adults are advantaged because they have publicly provided pensions, healthcare, housing subsidies, tax breaks, and other benefits less available to younger age groups. To add insult to injury, you must work to pay for their subsidized healthcare and generous social security payouts, which you are unlikely to see for yourself. Generations younger than the baby boomers will most likely live with more restricted economic opportunities and reduced social benefits. They will encounter greater costs than their parents faced for education, housing, and healthcare. The political system favors their parents. In response, many of the younger voters in the 2010s were turned off from voting altogether, voted for Bernie Sanders, supported Trump, or failed to get enthusiastic about a Clinton or Biden presidency. While many older, White males ached for the loss of "their" America and a younger generation felt it was not such a great America for them, the shared response was underlying cynicism and a deepening distrust in government.

Globalization and Its Discontents

Globalization is now shorthand for the constellation of changes that involved low wage growth for non-college-educated workers and the decline of industrial cities and regions across the Western world.[27]

The United States played a key role in establishing the post-Second World War liberal-democratic political and capitalist economic order. In 1944 delegates from the Allied countries met in Bretton Woods, New Hampshire, to establish a system to avoid the prewar protectionism that was the backdrop to the Depression and the rise of fascism. A new order was imagined around open markets and free trade. New institutions such as the International Monetary Fund, the World Bank, and a precursor to the World Trade Organization were established to coordinate the integration of national economies into an international system. Behind the agenda was a belief that greater global integration was more conducive to peace and prosperity than narrow economic nationalism. Initially, it was more a promise than a global reality. Communism still controlled large swathes of territory. And there were fiscal tensions as the new trade system relied on fixed exchange rates, with currencies pegged to a u.s. dollar tied to gold. It was only with the collapse of fixed exchange rates and the unmooring of the dollar from the gold standard in the late 1960s that capital could be moved easily around the globe, scouring the world to ensure the best returns. There was thus a profound shift in relative bargaining power away from organized labor, which was fixed in place, towards a more "footloose" capital. There was a consequent severing of the ties between the national economic interests of labor and the global economic interests of capital. What was good for General Motors (and its shareholders), and its factories around the world, was no longer so good for workers in the usa.

The freeing up of trade meant that goods once made in the usa could now be made in China and then imported into the usa. The result: a global shift in manufacturing as the industrial base moved from the high-wage areas of North America and Western Europe to the cheaper wage areas of East Asia—first Japan, then South Korea, and more recently China and Vietnam. The workshop of the world shifted. The poverty rate in China in 1981 was 84 percent; by 2010 it had fallen to 12 percent. The global shift meant a redistribution of global incomes away from the blue-collar workers in the West.

The decline of socialism meant that there seemed to be no political or economic ideology that could compete with the reliance on free trade and open markets. No alternative was presented to the general public by the political and economic elites in the West who argued that free trade, global markets, and production chains that snaked across national borders would eventually raise all living standards in the long run. There was a growing chasm between these elites and the mass of unconvinced blue-collar workers. The backlash against economic globalization is most marked in those countries such as the United States where weak social safety nets and limited investment in job retraining or education compound the misery of economic dislocation.

The flattening of the world also allowed greater immigration and cultural flows that created a more diverse ensemble of cultural forms in terms of cuisine and movies, for example, and other forms of entertainment, values, and lifestyles. Cosmopolitanism was embraced by many of the elites but feared by others and used by some to gain political power. The foreign Other became an object of fear and resentment. The backlash against cultural globalization is evident in the rise of religious fundamentalism and political nationalism. Traditional religion became a refuge from the ache of modernity; a revived nationalism resisted the entry of the foreign Other. An idealized past was contrasted with the seeming cultural chaos of today. National culture was represented as under attack from outside and from the foreign Other here at home. Immigration is the most profound form of cultural globalization, and it resulted in a backlash in the USA as some of the White native-born Americans saw themselves as victims of globalization and displaced from their default power by the identity-seeking, opportunity-chasing Other. These fears were mobilized and heightened by the Trump campaign.

"Globalization" is now a catchword used to encompass the rapid and often disquieting and disruptive social and economic changes of the past 25 years. It contains much that was once desirable: improvements in living conditions through encouraging global trade, reducing conflict and the threat of war through political alliances, and encouraging cultural diversity in an ever-closer world. At its best globalization closes the distance between places and people, but its downsides include loss of jobs and growing economic insecurity. Even as inequity intensified and the middle class suffered, the Democratic administrations of Clinton and Obama pursued a globalizing economic agenda. If the Republicans had a trickle-down theory that presumed— despite all the evidence to the contrary—that making the rich richer benefits everyone, the Democratic equivalent was that the benefits of globalization would benefit everyone. In fact, it negatively impacted the bottom 50 percent.[28] Many of the workers felt ignored by Democrats, who promoted an economic globalization that undercut their jobs and a cultural relativism that undermined their values.

Many of those who felt shamelessly used by the Republicans and shabbily treated by the Democrats turned to more insurgent candidates such as Obama and, latterly, Trump. As the scion of a millionaire family, he was not quite the obvious standard-bearer of the economically marginalized, but his outsider status and maverick campaign resonated with a substantial mass of Americans. He was particularly successful in the Rust Belt, winning states that Obama had previously won, including Iowa, Michigan, Minnesota, Ohio, and Pennsylvania, as well as Florida and North Carolina.

Globalization in its present form has generated economic inequalities, political uncertainties, and cultural anxiety. In the United States, as elsewhere, it created the breeding ground for the rise of economic nationalism, authoritarian populism, and conspiratorial narratives. The United States was a particularly fertile soil for these movements to flourish.

3

A Flawed Democracy

Each year, *The Economist* publishes a Democracy Index. The 2022 edition listed 167 countries ranked on metrics of five dimensions: electoral process and pluralism, the functioning of government, political participation, democratic political culture, and civil liberties. The United States ranked 26th in the world. At the top of the list were Norway, New Zealand, Finland, and Sweden. At the bottom were North Korea, Myanmar, and Afghanistan. No real surprises there, but Taiwan (8th), Uruguay (13th), South Korea (16th), the UK (18th), and Costa Rica (21st) all outranked the USA, which over the past six years had slipped five places and from a full democracy to a flawed democracy.[1]

All democracies have flaws. They are human creations after all. But the United States has more flaws than many of its democratic peers. And as the events of January 6, 2021, revealed, there is a disturbing rise in the refusal by some in the country to accept the results of its democratic elections. I want to explore some of the reasons behind this democratic slippage. In this chapter, I focus on electoral issues rather than the deep-seated socioeconomic context of the insurrection.

It is important to begin with the realization that the United States was founded as a republic, not as a democracy. The founders were distrustful of the raw political energy of the people. In 1787, James Madison described democracies as "spectacles of turbulence and contention . . . incompatible with personal security or the rights of property."[2] Government in the early Republic was structured to insulate political elites from popular opinion. The Congress and the other two branches, the executive and the judiciary—a nine-member oligarchy of lifetime political appointees whose guiding ideology always seems half a century behind the general public's—limit and blunt the expression of the popular will. The hallmarks of a healthy democracy are that each vote should be counted and each one should count equally. This is not the case in the USA, where the disparity between popular will and political representation is growing. Let's look at four sources of the growing deficits of u.s. democracy.

Follow the Money

Money plays a huge role in u.s. politics. Members of Congress need to solicit vast amounts of money to wage their electoral campaigns, and these funds come from a variety of sources: the modest contribution of the ordinary citizen that can sometimes make a difference in insurgent campaigns, the legal contributions from well-funded groups, and the "dark money" of nonprofits, which include unions, trade organizations, and political action committees (PACs), which do not have to disclose their donors, since individuals can contribute to these organizations' political campaigns while remaining anonymous. The Supreme Court, in a series of rulings including *Buckley v. Valeo* in 1976 and *Citizens United v. FEC* in 2010, made it easier for all types of money, including dark money, to flood into the political system.

Politicians look to garner support through campaign contributions. Just one example: In May 2021, the FBI was investigating a case involving Susan Collins, a U.S. senator and Republican from Maine, for receiving contributions to her 2020 reelection campaign from an organization run by an executive at the defense contractor firm Navatek. Senator Collins sits on a key Senate subcommittee that controls military spending. In 2019, Senator Collins lobbied for Navatek to receive an $8 million contract at a Maine shipyard. In the 2020 election, the Navatek executive routed $45,000 personally and $150,000 through a PAC to support her reelection bid.[3]

Collins is not accused of any wrongdoing. It is the executive who is under FBI scrutiny, for allegedly breaking one of the few legal restrictions on campaign contributions: being a defense contractor and giving a political campaign contribution. Collins, in contrast, did nothing wrong, legally speaking. She could be said to be working for the constituencies in her state by directing work to a shipyard in Maine. There is no obvious personal venality by Collins. While individual politicians such as Collins may not be corrupt in the formal sense of gaining personally in exchange for a service or favor, the system is rotten to the core. Many political campaign contributions that would be deemed illegal in most of the other liberal democracies around the world do not constitute corruption in the USA. They are a normal part of everyday politics, business as usual.

Today, policies in Washington, DC, are shaped more by interest groups who hone regulations to meet their needs, rather than the needs of the ordinary electorate. The political system listens to money, a commodity politicians desperately need to stay competitive in campaigns, win electoral races, and remain in power.

Those with the most money have the best access: they have the power to influence and advise. Ordinary people exercise political choice at elections but those with money exercise real political power all the time.[4]

Divided Government

Under the mounting pressure of growing partisanship, the constitutional division of political responsibilities across the different levels of government is now revealed as a major flaw.

The rigging of the voting system for the u.s. Senate so that some electoral votes count more than others is not new; it's a foundational reality, an integral part of the political architecture of the country. Under the u.s. Constitution, each state receives the same number of senators, despite differing population sizes, while the number of representatives afforded to a state is based on its population. This rule started at the beginning of the Republic, when each state was allocated two senators. At the time of the First Congress in 1789 the populations of the largest and the smallest state—Virginia and Delaware, respectively— were 110,936 and 11,783 (bearing in mind that we only include free White males over sixteen years old in these figures, as befits the prioritization of the time). Roughly, a ninefold differential. By the time of the 2016 presidential election, the populations of the most and least populous states, California and Wyoming, respectively, were 39.25 million and 585,501. The differential has increased to 67-fold, while the senator allocation has remained the same. Senators from small states with reliably consistent voting preferences can amass seniority that bestows enormous power beyond their demographic significance. A longtime leader of the Senate, Mitch McConnell, co-represents a state with a total population of only 4.4 million and that is 89.4 percent White with only 3.5 percent foreign-born, while the u.s. average is 71.7 percent White and 12.9 percent foreign-born.

Senate representation reflects the political realities of largely rural eighteenth-century America rather than the demographic realities of the metropolitan twenty-first-century nation it has become. More than one-quarter of the entire u.s. population resides in just ten metro areas across only sixteen states. And 85 percent of all Americans now live in metro areas. The opinions of the metropolitan majority on such issues as gun control, abortion rights, or immigration policy are countermanded in the Senate by the preferences of voters in small, rural states.[5]

Political power no longer parallels demographic realities. To be sure, the United States was never designed as a democracy but as a republic, one engineered to limit the power of the people and prevent political convulsions. The multiple sources of governmental power were to be a check on unbridled power. However, today, they tend to favor more rural and more conservative states. Members of the Supreme Court are appointed by senators representing a minority of the u.s. population.[6]

In contrast, seats in the House of Representatives are based on the population of the states.[7] Thus California, with a population of almost 40 million, sends 52 representatives to the House, while New Hampshire with a population of 1.4 million sends only two. However, the pooling of Democratic voters into dense areas lessens their effectiveness as they tend to win big in a few districts while Republicans have a wider national spread. The current system gives the Republicans an advantage at the national level. A mathematical model produced by *The Economist* concluded that the Democrats need to win 53.5 percent of all votes cast to have an even chance of winning a House majority.[8]

Although voting also takes place at the more local level of towns and cities, there is a problem: state legislatures can overturn local initiatives. Twenty-four states now have pending legislation to reverse ballot measures that were introduced at the local level. In Virginia, during Republican control of state legislature, the state prohibited localities from removing memorials or replacing street names that honor southern "heroes" of the Civil War. In this case, the democratic will of progressive districts was blocked because they were encased and countermanded by the power of a conservative state legislature. This power goes both ways, as conservative localities, albeit much more rarely, can be blocked by progressive states. This was evident in local resistance to more liberal states' mandates for mask wearing during the worst of the COVID-19 pandemic.

In the United States, it is the Electoral College, not the voting public, that elects the president. This system was established in the Constitution to blunt the power of raw popular opinion. It is not the total votes cast for a presidential candidate that leads to a winner, but the votes of the 538 electors of the College, allocated to each state in the same numbers as their congressional delegation. It tends to favor the large states, since they have more population and hence more congressional representation. From 1888 onwards, the system worked well in that the popular vote and the Electoral College were in sync. However, in both 2000 and 2016, a candidate won the presidency without obtaining a majority of the popular votes. If presidents were elected by a simple popular vote, we would have had President Hillary Clinton and President Al Gore. The Electoral College does not transmit the will of the people; in fact, it's starting to undermine it.

The Electoral College system also overvalues voters in large swing states, that is, those states with a more even split of Democrat and Republican voters, such as Florida, one of the usa's largest states and one with a diverse demographic profile. Florida's elderly voters, self-identified Jewish voters,[9] and anti-Castro Latino voters who conflate socialism/authoritarianism with more liberal social-welfare policies have influenced national policies as a succession of presidential candidates sought to appease these groups in order to win the presidency. u.s. foreign policy toward Israel and Cuba, and domestic safeguards to Medicare, are in no small part a function of the importance of Florida's Electoral College votes.

Gerrymandering

Then there is the manipulation of voting boundaries to engineer specific political outcomes.[10] The political party that controls state legislatures is directed by the Constitution to redraw congressional boundaries every ten years, after the results of the most recent Census, in order to take account of population shifts. This redistricting is often done to win seats and is known as gerrymandering. Basically, it allows politicians to select their voters, rather than citizens to choose their representatives. In 2012, Republicans won a majority of 33 seats in the House despite getting 1.4 million fewer votes than their Democratic opponents.

The term "gerrymandering" originates with the activities of Elbridge Gerry, who, in 1810 as governor of Massachusetts, signed a bill that created legislative boundaries that favored his political party. A cartoonist of the day depicted the outline of the boundaries as a salamander. The system was so "gerrymandered" that the Democratic-Republicans won only 49 percent of the votes but picked up 72 percent of the seats. Gerrymandering involves what's called the "cracking and packing" of voters by moving the boundaries of voting districts. Cracking spreads opposition voters thinly across many districts to dilute their power, while packing concentrates opposition voters in fewer districts to reduce the number of seats they can win. Gerrymandering has gotten worse in the last twenty years for three main reasons.

First, gerrymandering is effective in helping political parties hold power in the House. Since 1995, after forty years of uninterrupted Democratic dominance, the House is now more competitive. It is up for grabs, and gerrymandering has helped tip the scales. One political consultant, Thomas Hofeller, described by many as a gerrymander genius, was particularly effective in designing redistricting strategies for Republicans between 1992 and 2017. He realized early on that redrawing boundaries was one way to elect as many Republicans as possible. He worked for the Republican National Committee in drawing congressional maps after the 1992 elections in Arizona, Michigan, Minnesota, and Ohio. The gerrymandered seats helped the Republicans win the House in 1994. He subsequently advised Republican politicians across the country on how to redraw electoral maps to their advantage.[11]

Second, gerrymandering has become a much more effective tool in the last twenty years due to greater insights into voters' preferences. With sophisticated computer programs and ever more detailed information on voters' location and preferences, politicians can now crack and pack with surgical precision. Maryland's 3rd congressional district, for example, slithered and slid across the state to pick up as many Democratic voters as possible. With pinpoint accuracy afforded by the new technologies, the Democratic-controlled state legislature was able to create a Democratic majority vote. More than one-third of all votes cast in the state in the 2016 congressional races were for Republican Party candidates but Republicans won only one out of eight districts. But across the country gerrymandering favors Republicans. The Brennan Center estimates that the tactic provides at least sixteen seats in the current Congress, with extreme partisan bias most obvious in Michigan, North Carolina, and Pennsylvania and significant bias in Florida, Ohio, Texas, and Virginia.[12]

The third reason is that the Supreme Court has effectively sanctioned gerrymandering. In 1986, the Court in *Thornburg v. Gingles* ruled against a Democratic legislature's attempt to thinly spread, or crack, minority voters among seven new districts in North Carolina. The ruling helped create districts where minority voters were concentrated and aided the packing of voters in future cases. Later, a more conservative court in *Vieth v. Jubelirer* ruled 5–4 not to intervene in cases of gerrymandering. Predictably, partisan gerrymandering then increased without legal challenge, especially after the 2010 redistricting round initiated by the 2010 Census results. In *Shelby v. Holder* in 2013, the Court in a 5–4 ruling overturned key elements of the 1965 Voting Rights Act that protected voters' rights in the South. The ruling gave the green light for a return to partisan gerrymandering in areas of the country previously under federal scrutiny. In 2017, and again in 2018, the Supreme Court passed up numerous opportunities to declare gerrymandering unconstitutional. The Supreme Court's recent decisions have emboldened its practitioners even more.

Gerrymandering has a pernicious impact on the electoral system and on the wider democratic process. It encourages long-term incumbency and a consequent polarization of political discourses. In gerrymandered districts, politicians only need to appeal to their base rather than to a wider electorate. Gerrymandering remains an ugly fact of the u.s. electoral system that belies the claim to democracy. Gerrymandered districts produce safe seats and lock politicians into political postures that promote ideological purity and party loyalty over bipartisan negotiation. Primary voters in gerrymandered districts thus count more than the general voting public.

Suppressing the Vote

Of all these disturbing trends behind the decline of democracy in the United States, voter suppression—a foundational feature of u.s. politics—is the most insidious. Women and Black people were long denied the right to vote, and strict citizenship rules were often employed to marginalize recent immigrants. Voter suppression is a way for a White oligarchy to remain in power. Naturally, there has always been resistance. Voter suppression was often met by renewed efforts at securing voting rights that in turn stimulated new rounds of suppressions by traditional holders of power. We can briefly recount the political history of the usa as a series of attempts to suppress an extended franchise that in turn prompts resistance, which then inspires new forms of suppression. Let me flesh out this assertion with a more detailed exposition.

In the wake of the Civil War, during the Reconstruction era, traditionally dated from around 1865 to 1877, three major constitutional amendments were enacted: the abolishment of slavery (the 13th Amendment, adopted in 1865), the creation of citizens from formerly enslaved people (the 14th Amendment, adopted in

1868), and the extension of the right to vote to Blacks and other minorities (the 15th Amendment, adopted in 1870). Together, they constitute a "Second American Revolution." It was a struggle to ensure political equality in the old South, where racist attitudes were most strongly held. Despite the hurdles and difficulties, Black people were elected to state legislatures in a period of political emancipation. From 1869 to 1876, two Black men became u.s. senators and twenty Black men were elected to Congress. This political flowering proved short-lived, however: once southern states reentered the Union, they were freed from outside and military control and local White political elites worked to marginalize the active political participation of Black people.

Reconstruction was dead by the end of the nineteenth century. In the South, White supremacy was reintroduced and maintained by the suppression of the Black vote through poll taxes, literacy tests, and outright intimidation. In 1896, 130,334 Black people were registered to vote in Louisiana, but by 1904 only 1,342. By the early 1900s, only 2 percent of Black people eligible to vote in Alabama had cast their ballot. Political disenfranchisement was maintained by White Democratic voting registers that excluded Black voters from voting lists and enforced by the threat and constant practice of violence by local and state police, and paramilitary terrorist organizations such as the White League and the Ku Klux Klan. This period of "Deconstruction" lasted until the middle of the twentieth century. It was reinforced by absolute Democratic control in the South and the entrenched power of incumbent White, southern Democrats in Congress, chairing influential committees to suppress, deflect, or minimize civil rights legislation that threatened the White monopoly of political power in the South. There was no federal civil rights legislation from 1877 to the 1950s. The Supreme Court was an active participant in what one legal historian refers to as the process of Black people being "erased from national politics."[13]

A new civil rights movement emerged in the 1950s. The 1957 Civil Rights Act, the first such legislation since Reconstruction, established a civil rights section in the Department of Justice (DOJ) that employed federal prosecutors to pursue voting discrimination and created a federal Civil Rights Commission. Put forward by a Republican president, Dwight Eisenhower, the Act was weakened by the southern Democrats in Congress. It was the last time that Republicans favored federal oversight of state voting practices and Democrats actively resisted it, as alliances were shifting. Over time, White voters in the South drifted to the Republican Party and Black people overwhelmingly moved their allegiance to the Democratic Party. Agitation and protest resulted in the Civil Rights Act of 1964, which sought to end segregation in public places and discrimination in the job market. It also inaugurated a restructuring of U.S. spatial politics as the South began its eventual transformation into a Republican rather than a Democratic stronghold, and consequently the national Republican Party became a more overtly religious and socially conservative party.

The 1964 legislation also provided the platform for the Voting Rights Acts (VRA) of 1965, which proposed stiffer legal safeguards to ensure registration and voting for Black people. The VRA has evolved over the years in a series of amendments—most notably in 1970, 1975, 1982, and 2006—but at its core, it prohibited discriminatory voting laws across the land and identified areas of the country subject to special conditions, termed covered areas (essentially the South). Section 5 spelled out these conditions: any changes in voting laws or voting procedures in these covered areas had to be precleared by the DOJ or by the U.S. District Court of DC. The political space of the country was reimagined; across the country there was a greater federal oversight of elections that traditionally had been the sole responsibility of the states. It was a shift of the ultimate control of elections from the state to the federal level because there was a sense that at the more local levels, discriminatory practices were both possible and actual. While much of the civil rights legislation had broad and general goals such as eliminating job and housing discrimination, the VRA specifically targeted the reality as well as the promise of the 15th Amendment by removing persistent and pervasive political discrimination. The VRA is one of the USA's most successful pieces of federal public policy. In 1964, in Alabama, Georgia, Louisiana, Mississippi, and South Carolina only 6.7 percent of eligible Black voters were registered to vote compared to 60 percent of Whites. By 2010, the figure for Black people was comparable to White people. In 1960, only 4 percent of registered voters in Mississippi were Black, but by 1984 this had increased to 26 percent. With the implementation of the VRA, Black people's political participation has increased dramatically, reversing decades of exclusion from the political process. In 1964, there was only one Black legislative in the originally covered areas, by 2010 there were more than 230. Black political representation increased across the country.

Shelby County is an affluent county in central Alabama with a population of around 230,000, according to 2022 Census data. The Black population makes up 14.5 percent, while 81 percent is White. At the state level, Alabama has a Black population of 27 percent. In Shelby County, only 7 percent of people are in poverty, but that figure reaches 16 percent for the state as a whole. Shelby is an affluent, predominantly White county in a poor state that reflects the recent political history of the South shifting from solidly Democratic in the 1980s to overwhelmingly Republican. By 2010, every elected partisan office in the county was held by a Republican. In 2010, Shelby County took a case to federal court arguing that sections of the VRA were unconstitutional. The county lost its case in a federal district court, a decision upheld in a court of appeals. The case went to the Supreme Court in February 2013. The majority decision released in that busy end-of-session week in June 2013, and written by Chief Justice Roberts, ruled that Section 4 of the VRA (which identified areas subject to preclearance) was unconstitutional. Essentially, it freed local areas with a long history of pernicious racial suppression from federal oversight.[14]

In the seemingly ever-repeating cycle of voter suppression leading to resistance leading to yet new forms of voter suppression, we are now at the "third stage" of renewed voter suppression. Stung by Trump's defeat in the 2020 presidential elections, Republican state legislatures tried to suppress the popular vote with new forms of voter identification and registration. Freed from federal oversight, states and municipalities across the nation have introduced discriminatory practices, fueled by the myth of voter fraud—which, in reality, is a negligible occurrence.[15]

Voter suppression masquerades as a means of ensuring voting integrity, yet it is nothing more than a brazen attempt to suppress Democratic-leaning voters. Its restrictive practices include onerous ID requirements that favor the affluent, the disenfranchisement of convicted felons once freed from prison, and the limiting of early voting and absentee voting. There are also more indirect voter-suppression tactics, such as inequities in voting facilities. Voters in poorer districts that have majority people of color tend to have to wait longer in line to vote than those in affluent White districts as there are fewer places to cast a ballot. In 2020, the Texas legislature worked to pass a bill that would not allow voting on a Sunday before 1 p.m.—the one and only aim of this being to suppress Black churchgoers from going to the polls directly after Sunday morning services. Many of the church faithful in this state lack private transport, so Black churches often provide group transportation to the polls. The same bill also sought to restrict people driving non-relatives to the polls—a law change aimed directly at elderly poor Black voters who cannot drive or do not have their own cars. Voter suppression in various forms is not about combating voter fraud; it is a way for Republicans to remain in power, even as the electorate drifts away from supporting them.

★ ★ ★

Fully functioning democracies give voters a sense of participation in a shared experience. Flawed democracies, in contrast, prioritize some groups over others, dampen popular representation, skew the electoral process, feed resentments, stoke anger about fairness, and ultimately create fertile conditions for political polarization and conspiracy narratives. There is no simple explanatory step from noting mounting democratic deficits to explaining the insurrection of January 6, 2021. However, the flaws in U.S. democracy are significant background factors. Insurrections happen in the context of declining political legitimacy and growing discontent. While all voters get to exercise political choice, only some get to exercise real political power. As the undemocratic trends strengthen, we are likely to see more crises of political legitimacy and more expressions of raw political anger.[16]

4

Conspiracy and the Politics of Outrage

The events of January 6, 2021, had their origins in a long, slow burn due to growing inequality that in turn caused political polarization, a legitimation crisis, and the deepening cracks of a flawed democracy. This atmosphere, decades in the making, was superheated and brought to the boil in the presidential election year of 2020 by the COVID-19 pandemic and crises of policing, each set against the darkening character of political discourse in the United States. It is not incidental that the insurrection took place in the context of a seismic shift in the national mood as it slipped into a conspiratorial moment.

Conspiracy Nation

The United States has a long history of political hysteria and conspiracy theories.[1] In a prescient essay, published in 1964, Richard Hofstadter identified a "paranoid style" in American politics that he described as "the sense of heated exaggeration, suspiciousness, and conspiratorial fantasy."[2]

Paranoid political rhetoric is disturbingly central in American political life. It appeared in the very early days of the Republic and has continued ever since. The first president, George Washington, was largely given a pass. He was the father figure, the revolutionary hero, and the embodiment of the country. But soon after his presidency ended, in 1797, after a second term in office, the unity of the newly formed nation fractured. This was not just in terms of separate political parties with different agendas, of politicians debating alternative views on taxation and foreign policy, but the sense of outrage among politicians at the bad intent of the opposition. The parties believed their opponents were actively promoting the downfall of the Republic—they were deemed to be, in the ultimate of political othering, un-American. Them. Not us. The Federalists even described Thomas Jefferson, when he was president, as being in league with shadowy secret societies including the Illuminati and Freemasons, and suggested that he was a secret agent of the French and part of a secret cabal of Europeans who were plotting the downfall of democracy and overthrow of religion in the United States. The basic themes are repeated throughout the nineteenth century, with conspiracy theories against Masons and Jesuits, and later in the twentieth, against Communists, proponents of one world government, and Marxist socialists. Each conspiracy is fueled by what Hofstadter described as a "sense of dispossession" in a fast-changing America. Dislodged from comforting and often imagined stabilities, followers share a belief in a conspiracy organized by the social and cultural elites. The believers see the conspiracy in apocalyptic terms and themselves as witnesses at an important turning point in the fate of civilization. They alone can read the hidden signs and see the existential danger. And they alone can turn the tide. The important role of charismatic leaders is often central to such narratives. Conspiracies are an essential part of the American tradition. While we may only want to consider the enlightening and comforting ideas fostered by American propaganda, such as the democratic impulse or the importance of personal freedoms, a more endarkening and discomforting paranoia also plays a large part in the history of the USA, often taking on a more central role at times of rapid change, cultural upheaval, and social dislocation. We are in one of those times.

Other countries also have fierce political rivalries and occasional outbreaks of hysteria, but the United States seems to return to evil conspiracies and associated outrage with a regularity and a passion shared with few others. The precise focus of the conspiracy changes from Masons and Jesuits to Jews and Communists, from Illuminati to antifa and from communist sympathizers to child-molesting politicians. The evil people change but the conspiracy narrative marches on. In the 1920s influential people such as Henry Ford put forward the idea of a vast, global Jewish conspiracy. In the 1950s Joseph McCarthy led a witch hunt from the Senate against a purported communist conspiracy out to destroy the USA. The advent of a more pronounced globalization in the 1990s called forth conspiracy theories against globalists.[3] The right-wing televangelist Pat Robertson spoke out against a New World Order said to be ferrying its secret agents around in black helicopters. A Republican representative, Helen Chenoweth, elected in 1994, reported that many in her district in northern Idaho had even seen the black helicopters.[4] The sentiments echo down the years. Whenever you hear the term "Marxist socialist," you can hear McCarthy's attempt to smear his opponents. The Illuminati may have disappeared, but they have been replaced by proponents of one world government. Freemasons and Jesuits are displaced by child abuse rings of Democratic politicians. George Soros replaces the Elders of Zion.

Despite their bewildering variety, conspiracy theories share a basic similarity. They subscribe to the view that nothing happens by chance, nothing is what it seems, and everything is connected. It is a sealed world that leaves no room for happenstance, accident, or contingency. There are hidden forces at work that explain . . . well, pretty much everything. True believers do not inhabit the sometimes random and chaotic world most people live in, where full knowledge of anything is impossible to achieve and any intentionality is often undone by outside factors, randomness, incompetence, and just plain bad luck. Conspiracists inhabit a world where nothing is as it seems, and seemingly random occurrences are all linked together, driven by the intentions of evildoers.

Conspiracy theories abound in the wider world, but in the United States they have an especially fertile environment in which to grow and blossom. This is for four reasons. First, the United States, with its dynamic economy, inclines to what Joseph Schumpeter once described as "creative destruction." The idea was more poetically captured earlier by Karl Marx and Friedrich Engels in the Communist Manifesto of 1848 in the phrase, "All that is solid melts into air." A restless and dynamic capitalist economy creates a constant sense of dislocation and instability. Conspiracy theories offer an encompassing worldview that provides holistic meaning compared to the seeming epistemological complexity, explanatory confusion, and discursive anarchy that usually surrounds us. It provides a balm for the ache of the present. Conspiracies provide the comfort of a worldview that explains why you're in the position you are in life and vaults your role from economic and political irrelevance to being privy to understanding the secrets of the world. Conspiracies valorize the existence of the believers, as they regard themselves as chosen ones who can read the secret signs and are members of a like-minded community dedicated to saving civilization.

Second, there is a long-established and sustained anti-government rhetoric in the United States that can see an oppressive government at work behind even the most modest of reforms. In combination with a strong populism that sees elite and establishment ideas as suspect and dubious, some people can easily adopt the worst-case conspiratorial explanation for why policies are enacted. Third, the deep strains of religiosity that run through U.S. society can at certain times and places become tinged with millenarianism, which sees political events more deeply as a Manichean struggle between forces of light and dark, good and evil.[5] And fourth, the country's complex and mutating multi-ethnic citizenry can create, for some, a crisis of identity about the national character. Times of rapid changes in ethnic and racial composition can generate disquiet, fear, and anxiety.

All these factors can create a sense of instability, dispossession, and uncertainty, and provide a nourishing ecosystem for conspiracies. The factors that make America unique, such as its economic dynamism and multiculturalism, also make the country's citizens more susceptible to conspiracy theories and political paranoia. Paranoia is always there in the murky depths, feeding on resentment and envy, anger and displacement, disruption and instability, and is forever capable of floating upwards to enter the mainstream.

It is important to remember that there are actual conspiracies in established power centers. The Catholic Church protected sexual criminals among its ranks of clergymen for decades. Tobacco companies long denied the insidious health impacts of smoking and the medical profession provided the tobacco industry with doctors in white coats to promote specific cigarette brands. Car companies have sold vehicles known to be deadly and oil companies have worked for decades to deny the real causes of climate change. The u.s. government, like most governments, has lied to its citizenry. The Pentagon Papers and the Afghanistan Papers showed how American governments, during the Vietnam War and the War in Afghanistan, respectively, kept lying to the public about the conduct of the two deeply unpopular conflicts.[6] These conspiracies witnessed not only the attempt by those in power to shield embarrassing facts from the public but also their failure to do so. They were revealed by dogged journalists and investigative reporters working in a free media space. It is perhaps a paradox that we are more aware of failed conspiracies and their attempted cover-ups because of better media surveillance of malfeasance. Conspiracies revealed are one of the surest signs of a functioning democracy, but their revelation can also lead to growing mistrust of the government and growing disbelief in the democratic project. What distinguishes actual conspiracies from conspiracy theories is that the former have a basis in reality and can be uncovered through investigation. They were truth-tested because they could be truth-tested.

A Sense of Community

Conspiracies are a shared worldview. They may be neither correct nor coherent, but they can metastasize if they have certain attributes. They need to be simple and easily understood, with identifiable villains such as the Illuminati, Jewish bankers, proponents of a New World Order, and, more recently, bloodsucking, child-molesting Democrats. No need for complex ideas trying to explain shifting realities; the conspiracy theory explains it all. It also needs to be broad enough to appeal to a variety of groups. As Michael Barkun suggests, the most successful conspiracy theories have a generic ecumenical feel. Broad theories can appeal both to religionists, who see the unfolding events as the work of the Antichrist, and to secularists, who perceive what's taking place as the elites' quest for world domination.[7]

The conspiracy also needs some links, however tortured and tenuous, to a deeper reality. The theory may be wacky and perverse, but it must resonate with or address some anxiety. Since the end of the long postwar boom in the mid-1970s, the United States has experienced growing inequality, the hollowing out of the middle class, declining social mobility, and growing precarity for many people. The population is changing, with a more diverse demographic and composition of different races, and there are fierce cultural debates about religion and lifestyles. When people lose trust in the government, the mainstream media, and organized science, they search for alternative truths, alternative facts, and alternative realities in order to make sense of the world and feel empowered. Conspiracies thrive in these circumstances.

People who share in a conspiracy theory find a sense of belonging by forging a community, a larger group of like-minded individuals, within an alienating—or in conpiracists' minds, oblivious or self-centered—society. In an anxious, confused country, shared conspiracies can become a source of meaning and comfort for the sad, the mad, the confused, the angry, and the anxious. Michael Bender, a reporter for the *Wall Street Journal* who followed Trump's election campaign rallies for almost an entire year, wrote about the Trump diehards who regularly filled the rows closest to the podium. He describes them as mainly

White, retired, and lonely people who attended the rallies because they offered coherence and community.[8]

* * *

The sociologist Max Weber identified three types of political leadership: charismatic, bureaucratic, and traditional. Most leaders in democracies exhibit characteristics of all three, but Trump was unusual in his heavy reliance on charisma. He cultivated a sense of community for his supporters. For many Americans who felt isolated from society, Trump's charisma shone brightly, attracting them like moths to a flame. Rallies, loyalty signaling, and flattery inflation became hallmarks of his governing style and led to the production of a Trump cult.[9] In the Trump Administration and within the broader Republican Party, facts and data were not assessed for what they revealed but reassembled to promote Trump, who was reimagined not only as a political leader but as the special one, a guide leading the way through the darkness to the promised land. We can see the canonization of Trump in two communities: White Protestant evangelicals and QAnon believers. Let's begin with what at first blush looks like a surprising set of statistics. Trump's strong support among the former group ticked up from 77 percent in 2016 to 84 percent in 2020.[10]

Religion can be a counter to political partisanship. In many traditions it provides a set of teachings that value community, engagement, trust, and compassion; a rebuttal to the power of the market and the lure of partisan politics; a place to connect with others different from us. These traditions are all strong in the USA, one of the most overtly religious societies in the rich West. However, there is also a more partisan, overtly political character to some religions, especially Christian evangelical churches.

There is a reinforcing relationship between Republicanism and conservative Christianity, which are now so intertwined that, as political scientist Michele Margolis has shown, it is not simply that religious beliefs shape political allegiance but that political affiliations shape religious beliefs.[11] The relationship is now especially strong between the evangelicals and the right wing of the Republican Party. In 1976 Jimmy Carter received 50 percent of the White evangelical vote. But after 1980, once abortion and school segregation became major issues, allegiance shifted. White evangelicals as a self-defining category have a Christian theology with a distinct cultural and political identity that is now aligned with and informs a Republican right-wing agenda.

At first glance the evangelical and religious support for Trump would look like a stretch. A married man with two divorces to his name, a history of sordid sexual relationships, and charity contributions that on deeper inspection are self-serving vehicles: he would not seem the most likely standard-bearer for devout Christians. So, what lay behind the massive support of White evangelicals for Donald Trump in the 2016 and 2020 elections? American historian Kristin Du Mez argues that on closer inspection the connection between White evangelicals and Trump is transparent. She argues that his evangelical support was part of that group's long-standing embrace of militant masculinity, in which a strong man is considered a protector and a warrior. White evangelical support for Trump is not an aberration but the natural outcome of their beliefs. Evangelical leaders have long emphasized a militant masculinity that involved notions of patriarchy, submission, and power. While not all White evangelicals are so patriarchal, a dominant theme has emerged of the strong male figure as leader of the family and protector of the faith. Trump embodies this Christian muscular masculinity that is so central to their theology, although his own life is more about toxic masculinity than Christian masculinity.[12] The tradition of Protestant millenarianism is especially strong in today's evangelic community in the United States. For many, Trump represented a Christian militancy that they believed was necessary to counter the liberalizing trends in contemporary American society. The strongman president was protecting them from secularization.

There is also an emerging White Christian nationalism in the United States, an ideology that privileges White, Christian men. Sociologists Samuel Perry and Philip Gorski contend that Christian nationalism is now merging with a White nationalism that spouts replacement theory—that is, the fear that there's a conspiratorial scheme at work to replace White Americans with other ethnicities.[13] Since 2015, this theory has moved from the outer fringes to the mainstream. It regularly appeared in the rantings of former Fox host Tucker Carlson and is expressed by Republican politicians such as Senator Ron Johnson of Wisconsin and Representative Elise Stefanik of New York. The theory that an increase in non-White citizens is a deliberate scheme by liberals to sway the voting tendencies of the nation is now believed by about one-third of all American adults.[14] It was the guiding ideology of an eighteen-year-old gunman who killed ten Black people in a grocery store in Buffalo, New York, in May 2022.

The United States under Trump and in the lead-up to the 2020 presidential election was awash in conspiracy theories. One of the best known and most bizarre is QAnon. This conspiracy theory is based on claims about a "deep state" at work in the United States and the wider West, and, among other things, its proponents believe that there is a pedophile ring of powerful liberals at the center of American society. QAnon claims that there is a cabal—a favorite word of conspiracy theorists—of Satan-worshipping, cannibalistic child molesters that includes senior government officials, Hollywood actors, and Democratic politicians. But note, no senior business leaders. The theory does not question capitalism or identify capitalists as malefactors, only left-of-center political and cultural figures. Donald Trump, according to QAnon, was working in secret against this cabal to oust these nefarious evildoers and restore order.

The person at the heart of this conspiracy theory, known only as Q, was supposedly a senior government official with a high-level security clearance. (Q posted online anonymously, hence QAnon.) Q posted enigmatic messages that claimed Trump had a plan to prevent an Obama takeover and was diligently working to arrest the leaders of the cabal. There are other assertions, too many and too weird to go into detail here. Suffice it to say, QAnon had all the key elements of the classic conspiracy theory, where everything is connected and nothing is as it seems. Only the initiates could see the real patterns. The plan was flexible enough to accommodate anything and everything. Even the Mueller investigation into Russian interference in the 2016 u.s. elections was part of the plan. Trump only pretended to conspire with Russia to get the Mueller investigation started, because he was then going to use it to investigate the Democrats. Everything was happening as part of a grand plan. Trump's election loss was part of the plan too . . . until it wasn't. You get the idea. At the heart of the QAnon conspiracy theory was the idea that Trump was leading the resistance against the evil cabal and the struggle to destroy the deep state, and was engaged in the final conflict between light and darkness. The conspiracy leached out into wider society. Supporters with

QAnon shirts and regalia appeared in ever greater numbers at Trump rallies, and by February 2020, 29 percent of Republicans firmly believed that Trump was fighting against child sex traffickers. QAnon ideology blended easily into Trump's presidential campaigns. It was not a big stretch. He had long espoused the conspiracy of a "deep state." In the election year of 2020, he ramped up the claim and tweeted and retweeted QAnon-related messages over 250 times.[15] Images from the assault on the Capitol on January 6 clearly show the pervasive influence of the QAnon supporters. Many of those who attacked the Capitol wore QAnon shirts and sported its paraphernalia; many waved the QAnon flag. There were more Trump and QAnon flags there that day than U.S. flags. Many of those who marched on the Capitol, and millions more, subscribed to, and continue to believe in, the QAnon conspiracy.

The Permeable Membrane

The dean of conspiracy theory studies, Michael Barkun, describes what he calls a permeable membrane between the fringe and the mainstream. In 2016 he wrote,

> What was once clearly recognizable as "the fringe" is now beginning to merge with the mainstream. This process of "mainstreaming the fringe" is the result of numerous factors, including the ubiquity of the Internet, the growing suspicion of authority, and the spread of once esoteric themes in popular culture. Only a permeable membrane now separates the fringe from the mainstream. Thus, conspiracism is no longer the province only of small, isolated

coteries. It now has the potential to make the leap into public discourse.[16]

Since these words were written, the membrane has all but ceased to exist.

In the United States, the paranoid style is not a uniquely Republican characteristic. Democratic criticisms of the status quo can often imagine an all-powerful, all-knowing military–industrial–security system at work to thwart democracy. These ideas are often embodied in popular Hollywood movies, such as *Enemy of the State* (dir. Tony Scott, 1998) and many others. Antisemitic and anti-government rhetoric can cross traditional party lines. Oppressed groups also see conspiracies at work that reinforce their marginal status. While these are important islands of resistance to mainstream views, they do not necessarily enter the political mainstream. They remain part of what academic Patricia Turner describes as folkloric legends and rumors.[17] But in the United States, one of the only two main political parties opened the door wider to the conspiratorial. With only two parties to cover the full spectrum of mainstream political ideas, each party is like a large tent. Outside the tent, among the decent and honorable are also the wild and the wacky, the conspiratorial and the crazed. Most of the time they remain outside the bounds of the party or, if given entry, are only apparent at the fringes or the outermost reaches. But today, in a Republican Party that has often flirted with the marginal, the more conspiratorial ideas have found a uniquely significant and central role. Trump's populism, which alluded to conspiracies and evil forces at work, resonated with many people left behind by an American capitalism that was turning all that they deemed solid into air.

The extreme right, and especially the conspiratorial right, has always been a force in Republican circles, but it is a force that waxes and wanes. The Republican populist Joseph McCarthy legitimized conspiracy theories in the 1950s in a way that combined anti-communism and anti-intellectualism. The vehemently anti-communist John Birch Society was founded in 1958 and by the mid-1960s had grown to roughly 60,000 members. It was strong in Texas, Arizona, and California. One of its leaders accused moderate Dwight D. Eisenhower of being a communist dupe. Its influence was felt in the nomination of Barry Goldwater as the Republican presidential candidate in 1964. The Bush presidencies, in retrospect, mark a period when this extreme was moved to the periphery. The Bushes were not averse to playing the race card when it suited their purposes: There were the famous ads of escaped convict Willie Horton used in George H. W. Bush's 1988 presidential campaign to attack his opponent, Michael Dukakis, accused of being soft on crime. Later, in 2000, George W. Bush's campaign used racist imagery to undermine John McCain in the Republican nomination contest in South Carolina. But Bush senior cut his political teeth in Texas at a time when the Birchers were a powerful force. Fearing that they might doom Republicans to national irrelevancy, he was careful to avoid too rightward a shift in his own rhetoric or in supporting the Birch Society's political activities in Texas. The younger Bush, despite taking the country into an unnecessary war, externalized the evil Other in the form of Saddam Hussein and carefully avoided anti-Muslim sentiment at home. It is interesting to note, however, that a Manichean worldview was invoked by the Bush Administration in the early 2000s with the phrase "axis of evil," used by George W. Bush in his 2002 State of the Union speech.

The Republicans were defeated in the 2008 presidential election. Barack Obama defeated a Republican stalwart, John McCain, in a stunning outcome. For a very brief period, a matter of months, there was much Republican soul-searching. How could a Vietnam veteran be defeated by a political novice, a bi-racial Black man with few political accomplishments and limited political seasoning? Some Republican strategists pointed to a need to change the party's image. Relying on older White voters, they suggested, was dooming the party to irrelevancy in the face of demographic change. There was a very short-lived debate about making the party more open to immigrants and minorities and changing the party toward a more inclusive movement, because, before the change was fully discussed or could gain traction, the Tea Party Movement galvanized the base. In 2009, fed up with bailouts to wealthy bankers, the enlargement of federal govern-ment, and an unpopular war, a grassroots organization was born devoted to small government, limited taxation, and a burning hatred of Obama's domestic agenda, especially the introduction of healthcare mandates. It was the standard small government, anti-tax movement but lightly sprinkled with conspiracy theories and a touch of racist animus. It received funding from the right-wing millionaire Koch brothers and was given lavish airtime by Fox News, eager to undermine Obama's presidency. The Tea Party was not strong enough to become a third party in America's political system but was large and significant enough to shift the existing Republican Party rightwards. A congressional Tea Party caucus was founded in 2010. At its height, a year later, it had sixty members in the House and the informal caucus had twelve members in the Senate. Current senators in the informal organ-ization include Marco Rubio, Mitch McConnell, Ted Cruz, and

Ron Johnson. When the House Leader Eric Cantor was defeated in a Republican primary in 2014 it sent a warning of the power of Tea Party sentiment. The problem for Cantor was not that he was a moderate. He voted against any increase in the minimum wage and while parsimonious with help for working people, he never saw a private market interest that could not be helped with government support. He was one of those Republicans who practiced socialism for the rich and rugged capitalism for the rest. He was happy to bail out the banks after the global financial crisis but unwilling to help individual families at the time of crisis. But after the bank bailout in 2008/9, populist sentiment had to be addressed. The ideology of business now had to compete with the rhetoric of nationalist populism, which had been muted for decades. Cantor's problem was not his support for the business side of Republican ideology but that he was too slow to embrace the emerging populism that was beginning to take control of the party. It was a foretaste of things to come as his primary defeat was noted by Republicans seeking to obtain or keep a nomination. If even the most powerful congressional leader could be defeated by a right-wing challenger, no one was safe, and those who wanted to hang onto their seats needed to embrace the populist right. Trump's capture of the Republican Party is the consequence of, not the reason for, this rightward populist shift.

Much is often made of the uniqueness of Trump. He was often portrayed, especially by moderate Republicans, as an outlier, not part of the true Republican tradition. But that is to ignore a recurring theme in the Republican Party, the long tradition of "government mistrust, racial resentment, and conspiratorial beliefs."[18] Trump's race-baiting demagoguery is part of a long-established extreme right tradition in the United States and in the Republican Party. Where he was unique was in his success in tapping into conspiratorial grievances with his 2016 presidential election platform—one built on being an outsider to the Washington establishment and an enemy of the global financial elite. His overt playing to populist resentment and racial bigotry effectively allowed a greater space for conspiratorial theories to enter mainstream politics through the Republican Party.

Conspiracy theories are shared narratives. Today, they are easier to create, generate, and disseminate because of a wider range and deeper reach of media platforms. While many focus on social media it is important to remember the importance of traditional media to the spread of such ideas.

Talk radio was a major platform for conspiracies, the popularization of right-wing policies, and the promotion of Donald Trump.[19] Radio hosts such as Rush Limbaugh regularly voiced conspiracy theories. Talk radio grew out of the collapse of AM radio by the 1980s. AM radio had lost out to FM as the preferred medium for music broadcasting, and AM stations had a dwindling demand. One solution was to fill the airtime with talk and news programs. It was more talk and little news since authentic news-gathering is expensive, slow, and a cumbersome drag on profits. The partisan nature of talk radio was sealed in 1987 when the Federal Communications Commission (FCC) repealed what was known as the fairness doctrine, first introduced in 1949, which required stations to broadcast programming that was balanced. It required the holders of broadcast licenses to present issues of public importance by offering "different" viewpoints. The abolition of this doctrine is one factor behind the rising level of party polarization in the United States and the mainstreaming of conspiracy theories. After the ruling in 1987, stations could and did create entire schedules consisting of partisan commentary. Limbaugh was signed to his first contract in 1988. The national syndication programs sold only four minutes per hour for national ads and the remaining commercial time to local advertisers. So, the stations did not have to generate so many of the expensive national ads but could be sustained by reliable local advertisers. Within a few years of working at a small Sacramento station, Limbaugh's show was carried by more than six hundred stations around the country and then became the must-listen station for Republicans, especially elderly Republicans. Limbaugh had an estimated 20 million listeners a week for almost twenty years. He filled the airwaves with bile and resentment, stoking fear and anger. Limbaugh traded on conspiracy theories and generated an ugly divisiveness. He was a fervent Trump supporter and was rewarded with the Presidential Medal of Freedom in 2020.[20]

By the 2010s, talk radio was struggling with an aging listenership and declining ability to attract a younger audience. The two large station owners, iHeartMedia and Cumulus Media, who expanded their business by gathering up over 1,000 radio stations between them, filed for bankruptcy court protection in 2017 and 2018. But as talk radio was beginning its decline into demographic irrelevance, new platforms emerged to promote right-wing partisan ideas and conspiracy theories.

Cable "news" channels have proliferated in the last three decades, with the major networks establishing stations to appeal to different niches in the market. Historian Nicole Hemmer describes the rise of a new political–entertainment media complex that includes talk radio and cable news populated by a punditocracy that, especially on the right, espouses skepticism about democracy itself.[21] Today there is little real news on cable channel news stations. News gathering is an expensive, time-consuming business. It requires reporters and sources on the ground and sophisticated editing and production to tight schedules. BBC News, for example, has fifty foreign news bureaus and 250 correspondents around the world. At peak times any of these resources can be mobilized. In contrast, at peak viewing time Fox News had Tucker Carlson, a privileged White man who pontificated from a Washington studio while wearing a bowtie as a self-conscious prop to buttress a sense of wealth and intellectual sophistication, and who ranted about political correctness, immigrants, and at times exhibited a strange bromance with Putin and Russia. And, of course, he was against vaccines and was opposed to the 2020 election results.

Cable news is not so much about news but about keeping your audience. MSNC has a left-wing bias while Fox has a right-wing bias. They both reflect and reinforce the prejudices of their audience and they do so in the cheapest way possible. A single commentator will sit in a studio and talk with guests (some paid, most unpaid) who will dissect the day's "news." There is little in-depth coverage, just talking heads. With no need for balance, they will simply repeat an endless echo chamber. The channels espouse opinions and beliefs more than facts and information. Donald Trump was a boon to the cable news industry. The right loved him, and the left hated him. Both watched him. And no need to even interview him. He tweeted enough to feed the news cycle each and every day while he was president. Cable news was able to spend hours deconstructing his words with the intensity of theological professors unpacking the meaning of passages in the Bible. It made money for everyone and gave Trump hours of free publicity.

Cable news is a wide spectrum. At one end CNN had the resources and commitment to mobilize reporters and do some great reporting on fast-moving events in distant lands. At the other extreme was Alex Jones and Infowars. Jones had been peddling outrage since the 1990s with unhinged conspiratorial theories. He started out on a radio show in Texas with a steady diet of anti-government conspiracy theories. He claimed that the attack on the World Trade Center in 1993 and the Oklahoma City bombing of 1995 were false flag events—that is, not real events but stage-managed ones, pretexts for government control. In 1999 he established Infowars. He gained platforms online, including on social media—Facebook, Twitter, and YouTube. His influence grew with cable news channels, and the algorithms of social media enabled further growth by rewarding his outrage and extremism with greater dissemination. He had 30 million viewers for one of his documentaries. He made money by commodifying his appeal, selling T-shirts, DVDs, and dietary supplements. He repeated the false claim that Trump had also promoted about Obama, that is, that he had not been born in the United States and hence was an illegitimate president.

As Jones's audience grew, his claims became wilder. He claimed that the 2012 Sandy Hook tragedy—where a lone gunman targeted an elementary school and killed 26 people, twenty of whom were children aged six to seven—was a false flag event, a hoax. He argued that there were no deaths and that the parents seen at funerals were actors.[22] He connected with the very worst of populist anger and his audience grew as his claims did, becoming ever more bizarre. One political strategist took note. In 2015 the Republican trickster Roger Stone, chair of Trump's election campaign, was invited onto Infowars. On December 2,

2015, Trump himself then appeared on the show.[23] It was a mutually beneficial exchange. Jones received a measure of legitimacy as a result of Trump's presence and moved from the periphery to the center of political discourses, from crackpot to commentator. The interview sealed Jones's reputation as fringe shock-jock with connections, a powerful influencer. Trump, in return, widened his base. There was now a growing overlap between Jones's conspiracies and Trump's pronouncements. Jones had access to Trump, whose repetition of outlandish theories in the media ensured that crazy talk became the norm. Trump used Jones's claims and rhetoric to expand his popular base, and vice versa. The result of this symbiotic relationship was the movement of the fringe to the center and the growing centrality of conspiracy in the political mainstream.[24]

The rise of Trump parallels an Internet filling up with new media companies. Under a law introduced in 1996 to give some measure of protection to the fledgling Internet industry, companies had no responsibility to monitor their content.[25] Media behemoths such as Twitter and Facebook, with algorithms that rewarded outrage and anger, gave an unregulated new platform for the racist and the conspiratorial, the unhinged and the unmoored.

The extreme political polarization in the United States, the growing appetite for conspiracy theories, and the ease of Internet dissemination were even weaponized by the enemies of the United States. In the presidential election of 2016, Russian troll accounts actively pushed the idea that the Democratic candidate, Hillary Clinton, was a member of a satanic clique of child molesters. Putin wanted to hurt Clinton. He saw her as part of the anti-Russian political establishment in the United States that had stirred up trouble for him, challenging his authority in Russia and Russian influence abroad. She was secretary of state during the Obama Administration, when there were anti-Putin demonstrations in Russia and anti-Russian demonstrations in Ukraine. Clinton was an enemy who had to be punished.

Conspiratorial communities were able to organize and promulgate their views via the Internet. QAnon, for example, never had a formal organization. Its ideas were spread through the viral networks of the Internet. Even after the mainstream media companies sought to ban those who espoused QAnon, separate online chatrooms broke off from the mainstream platforms, with people moving their accounts elsewhere to continue to voice their virulent views.

Building on a long tradition of political paranoia, conspiracy theories have moved from the periphery to the very core of political discourse in today's USA. Such crazy ideas are not only more easily disseminated, but validated by powerful media outlets and influential public figures. The USA is now a fertile ground for conspiracy beliefs. The protestors on January 6 had been fed narratives and conspiracies that made their rush on the Capitol not only acceptable but, for some, absolutely necessary.

The Allure of Violence

In early December 2016, 28-year-old Edgar Maddison Welch drove alone in his car from his home in North Carolina to Washington, DC. On December 4, during packed opening hours, he entered a popular pizzeria on busy Connecticut Avenue brandishing an assault rifle. He said he was looking to save children from being held as sex slaves in the basement of the restaurant. He fired his weapon three times.[26]

Welch, along with many others, believed a conspiracy theory that had been circulating on the Internet that the pizzeria, Comet Ping Pong, was the center of a child abuse ring involving satanic rituals where children were tortured and raped by senior Democratic politicians. The idea had its origin in the hacked emails of John Podesta, an advisor to Hillary Clinton. Podesta's computer, along with other emails from the headquarters of the Democratic National Party offices, had been accessed by Russian operatives and released by WikiLeaks. The leaks were timed to distract attention from the release of an unflattering video of Trump spouting vile misogynistic comments. Conspiracists had circulated the narrative that the Democrats' emails revealed a sex abuse ring that used the language of pizza orders as code words for perverse activities. "Hot dog" and "sauce" were in fact code words for "young boy" and "orgy." Welch believed the conspiracy and traveled to DC from North Carolina to "self-investigate." Armed with an assault weapon, his intent was to save the children. In case you were wondering, there was no pedophile ring, no Satan worshipping at Comet Ping Pong or anywhere else on Connecticut Avenue. Welch was jailed for four years.

Two things (among many) are interesting about this story. The first is the use of a conspiracy archetype.[27] The narrative of Satan-worshipping child abusers is not new. In fact, it has a very long history. Jews in medieval Christendom were regularly accused of sacrificing innocent Christian children in blood rituals. Conspiracies that involve pedophilia all have the same basic structure through the centuries: a secret circle of people are discovered to be defiling the innocent and torturing the vulnerable; the accused are demonized by those who believe they are evil and need to be stopped; the narrative affirms the decency and solidarity of the defenders of the children and vilifies the "others," who at various times have been—and continue to be—Jews, women (described as witches), immigrants, and minorities of all types. The conspiracy alludes to such heinous acts to mobilize outrage.[28]

Claims of pedophile rings made an appearance in the contemporary USA even before QAnon and pizzagate. In the 1980s and '90s there were accusations that childcare centers were sites of horrific acts of violence and sexual abuse. One such hugely publicized case took place in California from 1984 to 1990, when members of the McMartin family, who ran a preschool in Manhattan Beach, were accused of having abused hundreds of children in secret tunnels. All charges were dropped after an extensive trial. In another case, in 1989, seven people who worked at the Little Rascals Day Care in North Carolina were accused of abusing ninety children. Graphic stories described abuse, torture, even throwing babies into shark-infested water. By 1995 most of the charges were dropped or successfully appealed.

These and other reported cases in the 1980s were part of a widespread "satanic panic," in which not only fearful citizens but police officers and investigators could see Devil-worshipping child molesters at work across the nation. Psychologist Richard Beck describes the satanic panic as part of a more general moral panic, one where the specific focus on day care centers was not accidental. Throughout the 1970s and '80s, more women worked outside the home than previously and traditional gender roles were being transformed. For many, it was a challenging and disturbing time, as the established family order seemed under threat. Day care centers for children were undermining the traditional idea that child-rearing was done by stay-at-home mothers. These social fears allowed a moral panic to gain traction, as well as find a target.[29]

What we are focusing on here is the use of child sexual abuse in a moral panic and its connection with more general fears of social change, where, as one commentator noted, "It's not really about the kids. It's about fears of a changing social order."[30] The Comet Ping Pong case was another iteration of a recurring moral panic, this time amplified by the Internet and reinforced by QAnon with the same archetypal elements, of tunnels, orgies, blood rituals, and Satan worshipping, but now directed to support Trump's presidential campaign.

A second interesting feature of the case is the use of violence. It is no accident, I think, that Welch was an American White man fed a steady diet of conspiracies. When he went to Comet Ping Pong with an assault weapon in his hand, he was acting out a very specific male fantasy. Numerous writers have commented on the current void of traditional masculinity.[31] Changes in the economy—especially a decline in living standards—as well as the cultural and social marginalization of blue-collar male work-ers all combine to question and undermine traditional notions of masculinity. To combat the feelings of being let down, ignored, and spurned by society, men like Welch think that "saving the innocents" is a way to take back control.

A toxic mixture of class resentment, gendered anger, and racial animus helped fuel the rise of Trump.[32] Strident White masculinity was a prominent feature of support for the QAnon conspiracists and it is no accident that most of the insurrection-ists at the Capitol were angry White men. It is also no accident, I think, that Welch, an American White man fed a steady diet of conspiracies, was also carrying a rifle.

The phrase "American Exceptionalism" was coined by Joseph Stalin to refer to the fact that the U.S. working class seemed resistant to the allure of communism. There was something in America that did not meet the rules of Marxist history. The phrase, first used as a criticism, was subsequently adopted as a mantra of celebration and patriotism by Americans. But there is something at the heart of the remark that's more than just a Stalinist put-down or boast. American exceptionalism has several characteristic features that make it distinct from its democratic peer group: more religious, less class conscious, more libertarian, more indifferent to economic inequality, less trusting of government. The social scientist Seymour Martin Lipset saw American exceptionalism as a double-edged sword, especially in its acceptance of inequality and its history of violence.[33] The USA is not unique in the democratic world in having a violent past. Europe, for example, has experienced both a thirty-year and a one-hundred-year war in its long history; its countries' imperialism violently dispossessed Indigenous people around the world; and it was the site of the killing fields of the First World War and the concentration camps of the Second World War. Most European countries cannot honestly recount their histories except as a recurring series of blood-soaked events.

Where the United States parts company with its democratic peers is in the more recent connection between violence and politics and the more central role of violence in national mythology. The country was born in violence as its early settlers annihilated Indigenous communities and then the colonists fought a war to obtain their independence.[34] Violence became part of the nation's sense of itself, part of its cultural fabric at home and a key element of its foreign policy. After the Second

World War the United States fought wars large and small across the world, from campaigns in Korea and Vietnam to invasions of Panama and Grenada, and more recently Iraq and Afghanistan. The United States is unique among rich democracies in its reliance on state violence abroad and having such high levels of gun ownership and violent deaths domestically. In the USA, violence permeates the millennialist undercurrent, is central to dominant forms of masculinity, and is a crucial part of national identity that is endlessly reproduced in cultural forms and personal belief systems. Violence, conspiracy, and outrage, as it turns out, are as American as mom and apple pie.

Many look on insurrection as a particularly unique blemish of Trump's America. There is an alternative reading, however, that sees insurrection as a troubling recurrence. The insurrection of January 6, 2021, was not the only such phenomenon in the history of the United States, which is studded with revolts and rebellions. The American Revolution (1765–91), Shays' Rebellion (1786–7), the Whiskey Rebellion (1791–4), and the Civil War (1861–5) all constitute a pattern of violent resistance to authority. Racially inspired insurrections occurred in the late nineteenth century. In the Election Riot of 1874 in Alabama and in the Wilmington (North Carolina) Insurrection of 1898, White supremacists refused to accept the results of legitimate, democratic elections, and installed their own segregationist politicians. The Wilmington Insurrection marked the end of Reconstruction and the full formalization of White segregationist power in the South. Other wealthy, democratic countries have experienced violence and riots but there is something distinctly American about assaults on the integrity of elections. There is a persistent dark side to the American experience of being in the world. A survey conducted by the *Washington Post* at the University of Maryland in 2021 found that one in three Americans believe that violence against the government can sometimes be justified.[35]

Toxic Populism

In the past fifty years, the very idea of America has been reframed and restructured, confusing and alienating many of its citizens. A toxic populism has emerged, arising from a sense of humiliation, cultural marginalization, economic decline, and political impotence in a polity of mounting polarization and growing extremism. It is tied up with distrust of the state and attracted to the allure of violence. The Internet and social media platforms made it possible for a poisonous mix of conspiracies to spread fringe ideas into the mainstream. Conservative news outlets did not just provide an alternative to liberal ideologies, they provided a counter-narrative to reality.[36] The toxicity increased as the two Trump presidential campaigns were supported by political extremists and marked by the acceptance of conspiracy theories.[37] Trump mainstreamed the fringe, making it central to Republican ideology and part of the national discourse. One in five Americans, according to an NPR poll, believe Satan-worshipping, child-enslaving elites seek to control the world.[38] It is as if, according to one conservative columnist, the "total indifference to evidence is today's American exceptionalism."[39] Many forces were at work that laid the foundation for the insurrection of January 2021, but toxic populism was one of the most powerful, pervasive, and significant.

5

The Year Before: Pandemic and the Crises of Policing

Although the insurrection occurred in January 2021, the forces stoking it had been building for some time. There was the long-maturing legitimation crisis and the steadily mounting deficits of a flawed democracy.[1] Two events in 2020 reinforced these longer-term trends. The pandemic and the crises of policing stretched the social fabric and tested the resilience of civil society. In early 2020 the nascent pandemic raised fundamental issues about the proper boundaries between public health mandates and individual rights. The debates that arose about enforced mask wearing inflamed conspiratorial movements. The summer that followed was one of discontent, with street demonstrations and public clashes in the wake of widely disseminated images of police brutality.

The Pandemic

At the start of 2020 Trump and his supporters thought, with some confidence, that he had a very good chance of being reelected to the presidency. The stock market was booming, and unemployment was low. The country faced few obvious external threats. The long war in Afghanistan was coming to an end. Leading

Democratic contenders such as Joe Biden failed to ignite popular support among the undecided. To be sure, there were some troubling events for the incumbent president. Impeachment hearings, ongoing scandals about payments to porn stars, questions about his finances, and inquiries into dealings with Russia all cast a pall. But in Trumpworld, which had achieved such complete cognitive capture of the Republican Party and of a significant section of public opinion, these were easily brushed aside and failed to undermine his bedrock support. At the very start of the year, things looked good for the president's chance of a successful reelection.

The first case of COVID-19 in the USA was confirmed on January 20, 2020, in Washington State, after a man had returned to the States from Wuhan, China. On January 28, 2020, the president's national security advisor told him that the recent viral outbreak in China could pose a great security threat, perhaps the greatest of his presidency. The deputy national security advisor went on to compare its potential impact to the influenza pandemic of 1918, which infected one-third of the world's total population. Warned of the possible impending catastrophe, Trump chose to play it down, annoyed that it might interfere with his reelection bid.[2]

At the beginning, the virus diffused slowly. By the end of February, there were still only fourteen detected cases. The first recorded case of local transmission that involved neither travel to an outbreak area nor contact with anyone diagnosed with the virus occurred in California on February 26. Three days later, the first recorded death from COVID-19 was reported in the state of Washington. In February, a chain of transmission from China to Italy to New York City led to an outbreak along the East Coast. The virus now had a firmer grip. A national emergency was declared on March 13. Two days later, the disease was present in all fifty states. By March 26, the United States led the world in covid-19 cases. By May 27, the u.s. death toll passed 100,000. By September 22, 2020, as the presidential election approached, the death toll had reached 200,000.[3]

A useful metric to make meaningful comparisons is deaths per 100,000 population. It is not an ideal measure, since not all covid-related deaths are tabulated as such and there are differences in recording cause of death. Despite these caveats, it is a useful, if crude, measure. At the end of September 2020, Peru had the highest death rate at 110.48, followed by Bolivia, Brazil, Chile, Spain, and the United States at 62.5. The u.s. rate was similar to the uk rate of 63.2, but twice as high as Canada and six times higher than Denmark or Germany. For one of the world's richest countries, with an affluent population and sophisticated medical system, it was a dismal performance.

The u.s. death rate was higher than many other comparable countries. American exceptionalism was most apparent when comparing deaths per capita with similar societies. Starting in March 2020, both Europe and the United States started from the same small base number. By mid-April, the u.s. figure was double and by July, it was eight times higher. The comparison is starker when we consider the advantages of the United States compared to Europe. The pandemic hit Europe three weeks before the United States, theoretically giving America extra time to acknowledge the need for effective treatment and testing. The United States has a relatively young population compared to Europe's more elderly and hence more vulnerable population. The United States also has a less dense population than Europe, a factor that might have dampened the spread of the virus in the former. The u.s. region most like Europe in terms of population density, the northeast, had a third more excess deaths in 2020 than the worst-hit European country, Spain. The sparsely populated western United States had an excess death rate four times higher than more densely populated Germany. The price of being an American was a greater likelihood of dying in the pandemic.

Despite the early warning, the United States experienced the worst pandemic since 1918, with infection and death rates higher than those in many other countries. As the virus swept across the United States the pandemic revealed the incompetency and mismanagement of the Trump presidency when it came to the most basic requirement of any government: to keep the people safe from harm. The president publicly downplayed the virus, failed to promote the wearing of masks, urged early reopening of businesses, schools, and civic spaces, and undermined the recommendations of his most senior scientific advisors. In March 2020 he started to hold daily press briefings. They were widely panned as a public health disaster. He hawked bizarre remedies and even suggested bleach injections to kill the virus. The president did not wear a mask in public until July 11. The pandemic revealed an incompetent and chaotic government administration. Support for Trump began to crumble, but still held firm among his bedrock supporters, who initially denied the existence of COVID-19, fought against mask mandates, and rejected scientific facts about the transmission and avoidance of the virus. There was no virus in Trumpland. It was all a hoax perpetrated by left-wing radicals. Evolving scientific knowledge was jettisoned for quack cures and masking was portrayed as an assault on personal liberties, rather than an act of sound public health. The Trumpland media encouraged COVID denial. Mass meetings of the unmasked were encouraged. It was a failure of governance of almost criminal proportions.[4]

The pandemic was a global tragedy that played differently in different countries. In the United States, as elsewhere, it highlighted deep, long-lasting issues, such as a declining public health system that was more geared to making money than providing healthcare for all; hyperpartisanship; attacks on and skepticism of science; and an administration that was more concerned about how Trump was portrayed than how well the American public was protected. The glaring cleavages in u.s. society were highlighted by the pandemic, which revealed yet again the injustices of class and race in the body politic. These failures were even more stark given the stunningly impressive feat of public–private efforts that combined government funding with private scientific research to create highly effective vaccines in little less than a year from the virus being first identified. It was not the government that failed, but the presidential administration.

Other countries also had vaccine deniers and conspiracy theorists, but the United States had a stronger cult of individualism and an associated distrust of the state. It also had an administration, a major news network, and one of the two major political parties effectively supporting vaccine deniers and undermining effective public health policies. The emphasis on individual rights that emerged in the early Republic was meant to form a zone of protection against the incursions of a distant monarch. Rights were promoted over obligations. Even as early as the 1830s, the French visitor Alexis de Tocqueville remarked that he found individualism particularly strong in the United States. He was critical of its pervasive quality and described it as a withdrawal from community and from the responsibilities of public life and citizenship.[5] Fast-forward almost two centuries and the United States is still dealing with the problems of promoting responsible citizenship. The fetishization of individual rights was most apparent during the COVID-19 pandemic in the decision on whether to wear a mask in public. Many of those who chose not to wear a mask, despite scientific advice, staggering death rates, and news of overwhelmed hospitals, said it was their right as an American not to. All number of commentators and bloggers saw the government health officials' request to wear a mask as an abrogation of their individual rights. It is an understanding of society as a collection of individuals—whose only responsibility is to their own subjectivity—constituted only by private desires.

Adding to the uncertainty of it all, there was also substantial confusion in the early months about the most effective public health measures as scientists and public health officials struggled to make sense of an evolving public health crisis. The ideology of individualism and the distrust of government made it more difficult for states, counties, and cities to impose lockdowns and pass mask mandates. There are no easy answers to if or when to initiate a lockdown. There was no clear scientific consensus and lots of unanswered and unanswerable questions in the very early days of the pandemic. Will a lockdown be effective and for how long? Too short and the virus may reestablish a strong hold. Too long and the economic costs mount alarmingly. There are tremendous costs to closing businesses or conducting education online that cannot be easily dismissed. And often the costs are regressive, with the most vulnerable paying the highest price. There were difficult decisions and lots of gray areas, but the United States had a hard time even accepting minimal public health measures if they impinged on individual behaviors.

The pandemic provided a civics lesson. We require people to do all manner of things that restrict choice if there is a clear and recognizable public good. We require people to wear seatbelts, take out car insurance, and stay seated when a plane takes off or lands. We put restraints on individual behavior for the public good. We are restricted in where we can dump our rubbish, how fast to drive, even how to discipline our children. We are not free-floating individuals kept aloft by our subjective preferences. We are members of a society with rights and obligations. Resistance to mask wearing in public during the pandemic was not restricted to the United States, but few other countries have imbibed two centuries of an ideology of individual rights to bolster their case and to promote selfishness and irresponsible behaviors as a key principle of what it means to be free. American individualism was an obstacle to wider mask wearing in the United States, and the result was one of the highest death rates in the world.

The pandemic and the ongoing debate about government-mandated lockdowns and mask use increased stress and anger in the country. More people than usual reported symptoms similar to post-traumatic stress disorder because of stay-at-home orders, restrictions on movement, deaths of loved ones, and fear of contact with coronavirus. There was a collective trauma that impacted on community cohesion. The pandemic reinforced political differences and calcified political partisanship. The individualist ideology of the United States, which is one of its abiding strengths, also makes it difficult for communities to coalesce around contentious public health measures. And in a time of hyperpartisanship almost all public health proposals were contentious. The pandemic, rather than bonding society, reinforced the lack of social cohesion and hardened political differences. The pandemic superheated the already fractious political divisions in the country.

Numerous studies noted mounting levels of anger, fear, and grief as the pandemic swept across the country in 2020.[6] Existing stressors such as poverty, debt, and unemployment were all exacerbated by COVID-19. Precarity was reinforced by the number of people who lost jobs, incomes, friends, and family. The pandemic created a growing sense of dislocation. Throughout history, pandemics have ruptured societies amid factional scapegoating and divisive blaming of others. The more trauma people suffer, the more likely they are to turn to forms of extremism for support. In the years after the 1918 flu pandemic, for example, the areas of Germany that experienced the highest death toll also saw dramatic increases in voting for the Nazi Party. Influenza mortality rates in Germany from 1918 to 1920 correlate with the share of votes received by extremist parties. The experience of high rates of mortality led to increased support for extremist parties in the elections of 1932 and 1933.[7]

Susan Sontag suggested that plagues are invariably regarded as judgments on society requiring some form of response.[8] For every plague, there's a culprit. The pandemic led to more recruitment by violent extremists, more conspiracy theories, and increased radicalization.[9] The pandemic brought economic ruin, social dislocation, and the loss of confidence around the world in all institutions, especially government. This was especially marked in the United States, where there was less social cohesion, a stronger resistance to government, and an established far-right ideology to begin with that was able to connect with many people's fears of social control and loss of liberty. The pandemic tapped into existing anxieties, and the Internet allowed people to band together in their search for answers. In a nation riven by a deadly pandemic, people searched for community at a time of social isolation. Communities of conspiracy emerged.

The American militia movement, which draws on the American Revolution as a model and as a justification for citizen resistance to a tyrannical government, is driven by a belief that there is a deep state at work to undermine the personal liberties of u.s. citizens. Michigan has a history of armed vigilante-style groups espousing such conspiracy theories. The Michigan Militia was formed in 1994 in response to perceived threats of government overreach into personal liberties. Precise numbers are hard to come by, but membership probably peaked in the mid-1990s with almost 10,000 members, including Timothy McVeigh and Terry Nichols, who were found guilty of organizing a truck bomb explosion at the u.s. Federal Building in Oklahoma City in April 1995. One hundred and sixty-eight people were killed in the explosion. The attack came as a shock to an American public more used to threats from abroad than from White, homegrown terrorists. Some years earlier, in February 1993, a bombing attack was carried out by Islamic terrorists on the World Trade Center in New York City. It had reinforced the equation of the "foreigner" being a threat, being "other" and "evil." In contrast, few were aware of domestic, White, right-wing terrorists. Soon after the execution of McVeigh and the lifetime imprisonment of Nichols, the fear of domestic terrorism again receded from view. Later, the terrorist plane attacks on the World Trade Center and the Pentagon on September 11, 2001, completely shifted any remaining attention from domestic to foreign threats.

In Michigan, the Democratic governor Gretchen Whitmer was criticized for announcing lockdown measures intended to contain the pandemic. In April 2020 thousands gathered at Michigan's state Capitol to protest the mandates. Confederate flags were clearly visible and some in the crowd carried automatic weapons and were dressed in military-style uniforms. It was a militarization of civil protest. Trump tweeted to his many supporters, LIBERATE MICHIGAN. A machine-gun-toting militia, the Wolverine Watchmen, an extreme right-wing militia group that espoused racial hatred and traded in conspiracies of a deep state, were regular attendees at the anti-lockdown and Trump rallies. They were just one of many recent militia groups to emerge as defenders of a citizenry against an overbearing government. Their presence at the state Capitol in full tactical gear was meant to intimidate, and it engendered an atmosphere of threat and violence. Members of the Wolverines took their resistance further than most. Through the summer and fall of 2020 they practiced drills and weapons training. They scoped out the governor's vacation home and planned to abduct her before the November election and take her as a hostage to an undisclosed location in Wisconsin to be put on "trial." Three were found guilty of the attempted kidnapping.[10]

The pandemic unsettled and disturbed an already divided nation and allowed more space for violent extremist groups such as the Wolverine Watchmen, who took on roles as defenders of the people against a deep state. Resistance to the public health mandates among the general public in the face of the pandemic gave an opportunity for extreme right-wing militias to emerge from the shadows. The militias were supported by a president who seemed not to apprehend that encouraging the violent can lead to violence. The January 6, 2021, insurrection was not an isolated event. The planned kidnapping and possible execution of a state governor earlier in 2020 was an inkling of the rage and anger emanating out of certain small pockets of the country, an early warning of the existence of a dangerous minority that believed that any government not headed by Trump was a form of tyranny that had to be overthrown. It was a foreshadowing of things to come.

Racial Reckoning and the First Crisis of Policing

On May 25, 2020, police in Minneapolis stopped a 46-year-old Black man, George Floyd. Accused of using a counterfeit $20 bill at a local convenience store, he was arrested, handcuffed, and pinned face down to the ground. As bystanders recorded the scene on their cellphones, the senior officer of the four arresting officers, Derek Chauvin, a White man, knelt on Floyd's neck. Chauvin kept his full weight on Floyd's neck even after Floyd pleaded that he could not breathe. Floyd stopped talking and after three minutes lay limp on the street. Chauvin kept his knee on Floyd's neck for six minutes more. This was not a violent struggle. The police officer's face showed a steady, remorseless countenance as he knelt on his victim, ignoring desperate pleas from Floyd and the assembled bystanders. Chauvin remained in this position long after Floyd had stopped moving and ceased to pose any sort of threat. Floyd died face down in the street, Chauvin's knee still on his neck. The recorded images that went viral looked to the entire world like a slow-motion extrajudicial execution by a White police officer of a Black man for a trivial, non-violent offense.

There is both a short, shallow narrative and a longer, deeper story to this event. The former is that all four officers were soon after fired. Chauvin was later convicted of murder and sentenced to more than 22 years in prison. The three other officers were found guilty of violating Floyd's constitutional rights and sentenced to two-to-three-year jail sentences. The city of Minneapolis paid $27 million in a wrongful death suit to the Floyd family. The short story, then, is a heinous crime was committed but justice was served.

The longer story is tied up with racism in the United States and its crisis of policing. Race plays a significant role in the history and present state of the country, founded as it was, after all, on the backs of human slaves, and with oppression and servitude as central features of its early economic, social, and political life. Black slave labor was used to dig canals, drain swamps, harvest crops, clean homes, look after children, pick cotton, plough fields, erect bridges, and build cities. As writer Ta-Nehisi Coates says, "they transfigured our very bodies into sugar, tobacco, cotton, and gold."[11] As racial categories were invented and imposed in order to delineate the type of person America deemed a "citizen" and who could be subjugated for the benefit of the rest, policing was used to define, confine, and contain Blacks.

Hypocrisy abounded. Thomas Jefferson, the primary author of the nation's founding document, the Declaration of Independence, could write eloquently about freedom while also being a slave owner himself. The blatant hypocrisy made the Englishman Samuel Johnson write in 1775, "how is it that we hear the loudest yelps for liberty among the drivers of negroes?"[12] Jefferson, the man who wrote and signed his name to the statement "all men are created equal," owned, without any major disturbance to his conscience, almost six hundred slaves on his Virginia plantation at Monticello. He was not alone in his spouting of liberty while practicing slavery. Twelve of the first eighteen presidents of the United States enslaved people, and at least 1,700 representatives from across the political spectrum in the u.s. Congress enslaved Black people.[13]

The legacy of slavery lives on today, especially in the enduring and stubbornly embedded inequality across any measure of things in the United States. According to the u.s. Census, while Black Americans have a median household wealth of $12,780, the respective figure for non-Hispanic white households is $139,300. The legacy also lives on in the built environment, in the names of streets, cities, universities, buildings, u.s. military camps, plazas, and statues that honor slave-owners and apologists for slavery and remind us that the popular understanding of the nation often has a willful amnesia about the central role and searing reality of its past. The Capitol complex, a symbol of the nation, the seat of government, and the stage for the insurrection of 2021, was built by slave labor. When Trump told his followers to go to the Capitol, he was guiding them to a building complex constructed by the hands of Black slaves. The buildings and statues remain, but the slave economy and human labor that produced their wealth is ignored. We are left with the lifeless artifacts of slavery scrubbed of their human costs.

The racial order of the South was defeated in the Civil War, but, after a brief period of Reconstruction (1865–77), White power was reestablished in the face of federal indifference. A deeply racist polity was created. The failure of the federal government to implement any form of real reconciliation or historical accounting gave enough opportunity and discursive space for apologists to rewrite a national history largely cleansed of the stain of slavery. And in an ironic twist, a racist secessionist movement was recast as a Noble Cause, romanticized and indeed celebrated. The myth was so entrenched that just a few miles from the Capitol, across the Potomac River, a major artery in northern Virginia was named after Robert E. Lee, the military leader of the southern secessionists. Many White people in the region seemed to take it for granted, as if naming a major highway after a rebel to the Federal Government, within sight of the federal capital, was no big deal. And for many it wasn't. To say otherwise, before now, was to disturb an established order and question an accepted myth.

The United States remains deeply racialized. Race is not a stubborn biological fact but is socially constructed, malleable, and shape-shifting. As Coates noted, race is the child of racism, not the father.[14] Black people are at both the center and the margins of American life. Their enslaved labor made the country rich both in economic and cultural terms and yet they remain on the margins of its economic wealth and political power. This ambiguous position is most obvious in the relationship between Black people and policing. They are at one and the same time both under-policed and overpoliced. Homicides and crimes in predominantly Black neighborhoods do not receive the same level of care and attention from police forces that the figures warrant.[15] On the other hand, they bear a disproportionate burden of policing in the form of higher incarceration and arrest rates. They also shoulder a disproportionate share of police brutality.

Policing in the USA, as in many other countries, is closely tied to issues of race and violence. The enduring crisis of policing in America includes the sickening toll exacted on Black citizens by police violence. Some see the origins in the history of policing in the country. Police forces were established to protect life and property; in the colonial era and the earlier years of the Republic, property included Black slaves. Slave patrols were created to bring back runaways and prevent revolts. Policing was then and to some extent still is bound up with enforcing racial segregation and the political disenfranchisement of Black people. The killing of George Floyd was not a unique incident but part of a long history of police violence against the Black community. Historian Elizabeth Hinton makes the case that police violence is not the result of uprising in the Black community but the cause. She upends the traditional narrative of law enforcement as a response to community violence. This traditional framing provides the rationale and justification for police force as well as providing immunity from public accountability. She argues, in contrast, that rebellions are responses to decades of police violence. Social disturbances are not the cause but the result of aggressive overpolicing.[16]

Several features make policing in the United States distinct from that in other similarly rich and democratic countries. First, there is the issue of guns and violence. The United States is awash in guns and has cultural norms that allow and promote gun ownership and use.[17] With only 5 percent of the world's population, the United States has around 40 percent of the world's civilian-owned guns. The United States is the only country in the world where the number of civilian guns outnumbers people. Policing is embedded in a culture where guns are widely owned and part of a wider violent gun culture that can render even the most benign of traffic stops into a potentially lethal encounter. It is not only the wide level of gun ownership but the high levels of gun violence that distinguishes the United States from similar societies. Compared to its socioeconomic peers, the United States is a violent society. In 2019 the death rate from gun violence was

8 times higher than that of Canada and 110 times higher than the UK. Even compared to poorer countries the United States fares badly. To take one example, while Tajikistan has a death rate by gun violence of 0.18 per 100,000 population, the figure for the United States is almost 4.0, making the latter stand out as one of the most violent countries in the world, where more people die from gun violence than from traffic accidents. Gun violence is on the increase after decades of decline; it spiked in 2020 as the pandemic increased tensions and restricted the criminal justice system from imprisoning bad actors.[18]

Police forces have long been armed but since the 1990s we have witnessed their increasing militarization and weaponization. The U.S. military transferred over $5 billion of equipment, including armored vehicles and ammunitions, from its forces in Iraq and Afghanistan to police departments in the United States. Tactics used by police departments now include aggressive policing in the form of armed SWAT teams and no-knock home invasions. Since the 1990s, many police departments have adopted the broken windows theory. In outline, the theory suggests that failure to prosecute small infractions—such as panhandling or loitering—gives a message of indifference that in turn creates and encourages criminal activity to proliferate. The solution proffered is to aggressively go after people committing small, less violent infractions, such as jumping turnstiles on the metro, littering, or loitering, or those seen as acting under the vague description of "suspicious." Its implementation has been overwhelmingly biased against young Black men. Despite the rupturing of community relations, the policy increased arrest rates, often the main metric used to ensure and increase police funding.[19]

Police in the United States are armed almost all the time. They regularly employ use-of-force tactics that allow chokeholds, other violent constraints, and the use of firearms. Most are trained in a warrior culture that sanctions the use of extreme force. They are also more protected than most from the consequences of their actions. The legal doctrine known as "qualified immunity," introduced to protect public sector employees from frivolous lawsuits, provides legal cover for police violence. Police have also been protected because of a powerful law-and-order discourse. In a time of rising crime, politicians and much of the public were led to see the police as the thin blue line protecting them from criminal anarchy. This gave powerful leverage to organized police associations to demand better wages, and conditions covering oversight, firing, and immunity that make it difficult to prosecute police. In 1973, for example, the state of Maryland introduced a Law Enforcement Officers Bill of Rights, which gave enormous protections to police officers that included scrubbing the record of complaints brought against officers and ensuring that only other officers and not civilians would be the investigators of violent deaths at police hands.[20] The legislation received bipartisan and overwhelming support at the time, and later was copied by many other states.

There is no national police force in the USA. Nationally there are almost 18,000 separate police agencies that are controlled and funded at the local level. The federal government has limited oversight of local policing issues, with police forces closely connected to local jurisdictions. This means that police unions can and do play an enormous role in local elections, not only funding general campaigns on the law-and-order agenda but more directly in choosing candidates to support. The policing of police is also often at the discretion of elected local prosecutors who are often tightly bound up in close working relations with the police.[21] To take just one example: Ahmaud Arbery, a Black man, was murdered in Glynn County, Georgia, on February 23, 2020, after he was pursued by three White men while out jogging. Initially no arrests were made as two local District Attorney's (DA) offices told the police not to make any. One of the assailants had worked as a police officer and later as an investigator for one of the local DAs. A case was only brought forward when a video taken by a passerby, which showed the vigilante chase and murder, was released and received national attention. The initial failure to prosecute an ex-police officer revealed the downside of the too-cozy nature of very localized criminal justice systems.[22]

Small police forces often lack the economies of scale to provide well-paid, well-trained jobs. With poor wages and poor training, departments sometimes struggle to attract competent applicants and, if they do, they often lack the ability to turn them into good police officers. In North Carolina it takes 32 weeks of training to become a licensed barber. It takes only sixteen weeks to become a police officer licensed to carry a gun, along with holding the immense authority to use it. With little oversight, police departments can come under the control of bullies and racists. This is a process made easier by the nature of policing, a very closed culture that relies heavily on internal coherence and group loyalty, and often has a hard time outing bad actors and bad behaviors. The small police force of Yonkers, New York, for example, employs around six hundred officers. Between 2007 and 2020, 102 lawsuits were successfully brought against the police department and $5.5 million was paid out in settlements. At least ten officers were named over four times in separate cases. Police officers, however, were rarely disciplined. A DOJ investigation found the department gave little guidance to officers in the proper use of force.[23] Even using national training services—especially the unsupervised and unregulated companies—is not the answer. A *Washington Post* investigation of widely used national training services uncovered attitudes that saw Black Lives Matter activists as terrorists and Democrats as inciting violent crisis. Some of the trainers had links to extremist groups. Sixty-five members of the far-right Oath Keepers had worked as law enforcement trainers.[24]

At the very worst, local police forces that not only lack oversight but fail to provide proper training can become little more than protection rackets. In the wake of the 2014 police killing of Michael Brown in Ferguson, Missouri, the federal Justice Department initiated an inquiry into the police department. It found a pattern of unconstitutional stops and arrests, a consistent pattern of First Amendment violations, and use of excessive force in violation of the Fourth Amendment. The local courts, in cahoots with the police department, imposed substantial and unnecessary barriers to the challenges to municipal code violations and imposed unduly harsh penalties. Ferguson law enforcement practices, driven in part by racial bias, disproportionately harmed the Black residents. For all intents and purposes, Ferguson Police Department was a racially biased protection racket concerned more with generating income than stopping crime.[25]

To be sure, not all local police departments are racist nor are they criminal conspiracies. Police work can be tough and dangerous.[26] Police are often overworked and underpaid, and their duties stretched too far. They must deal, often without adequate training, with the more dangerous consequences of the failures of U.S. society. Armed police are often the first responders at heated domestic disputes or the ones called to deal with someone experiencing a mental health crisis, situations that can often be the setting of violent outcomes. The warrior training of most armed police often fails to enable the nuanced response needed to navigate and carefully handle circumstances involving vulnerable or mentally ill people. Almost 25 percent of deaths resulting from police involvement are of people with mental health problems.[27]

In almost every case the problems are heightened when race is added to the mix. Black drivers are more likely than White drivers to be stopped by police. It is interesting to note the disparities disappear at night, when a veil of darkness obscures the skin color of the driver.[28] Black people are also more likely to have their vehicles searched. And in the USA, while police need probable cause to detain an individual on the street or in their home, they have more leeway at traffic stops. Legal historian Sarah Seo argues that using police in traffic enforcement, given racial bias, means that minor traffic violations can more easily lead to violent outcomes. Being a Black driver carries more risk than being a White driver.[29] Two examples from too many: In April 2021, a twenty-year-old Black man, Daunte Wright, was shot and killed by a police officer. He had been stopped for a traffic violation and when the police officers discovered there was a warrant out for his arrest they tried to detain him. As he moved back into his car, a White female police officer shot him dead. She alleged that she thought she was just tasing him. She was found guilty but sentenced to only two years' imprisonment. Six years earlier a police officer fired a gun into the car of Philando Castile after a routine traffic stop for a broken taillight. His girlfriend, Diamond Reynolds, and her baby were in the front seat. She streamed the proceedings immediately after the shooting event. She remained remarkably calm as she stated that the officer had just shot four bullets into her boyfriend as he tried to reach for his license. The police officer who killed her boyfriend, in contrast, sounded rattled, confused, neither calm nor competent.[30]

Police in the United States use deadly force more than police in most other comparable countries. Black people face higher rates of arrest and are at greater risk of police violence that leads to severe injury and death. Between 1980 and 2018, approximately 30,800 people died as a consequence of police violence in the United States. While the United States accounts for around 4 percent of the global population, it accounts for over 13 percent of global deaths due to police conflict. Data from a 2021 study published in the medical journal *The Lancet* show that the death rate was highest for non-Hispanic Blacks (0.69 per 100,000 population), followed by Hispanics (0.35), non-Hispanic White (0.20), and other races (0.15). The total rate increased from the 1980s to the 2010s. Black men are now two and a half times more likely to be killed by police than are White men.[31]

Black deaths from police violence were a regular event before Chauvin knelt on Floyd's neck for 8 minutes and 46 seconds. But, with the introduction of inexpensive video cameras and later cellphones, police misdeeds are now more regularly captured and circulated. In early March 1991, the video of Los Angeles police officers surrounding a Black motorist, Rodney King, and beating him senseless with batons as he lay on the ground gave visual proof of police brutality. The images shook the nation and the world, and led to an uprising in Los Angeles that summer when the police officers, tried in a predominantly White locality, were found not guilty. The case was the backdrop for federal legislation in 1994 that gave the DOJ the authority to investigate police misconduct. Over sixty police departments have since been investigated by the DOJ.[32]

The death of George Floyd was the latest in a litany of deaths of Black people resulting from police violence. In 2014 Eric Garner was choked to death as he told police, "I can't breathe." He was being arrested for selling cigarettes on the street. The same year, a young boy, twelve-year-old Tamir Rice, was gunned down in a park in Cleveland, Ohio, by a White police officer who fired the shot as soon as he appeared on the scene. And in Chicago, seventeen-year-old Laquan McDonald was shot by a White police officer. In April 2015 Freddie Gray was arrested on the streets of Baltimore for possessing a knife. He was then handcuffed, bound by police, and given a "rough ride" in a police vehicle, a tactic employed to subdue prisoners on their way to jail. He died seven days later from injuries to his spinal cord. The medical examiner ruled his death a homicide. Gray's death led to major protests in the following days and nights. Maryland's governor declared a state of emergency and deployed the National Guard. None of the six police officers involved was found guilty. They were either acquitted, had the charges dropped, or a mistrial declared. Alton Sterling, a 37-year-old Black man, was killed by two Baton Rouge police officers. Terence Crutcher was killed by a police officer in September 2016 as he stood unarmed beside his vehicle in Tulsa, Oklahoma. In 2018 Stephon Clark was shot and killed by two police officers in Sacramento while speaking on the phone in his grandmother's backyard. Botham Jean was killed in his home while eating ice cream when an off-duty Dallas police officer, his neighbor, entered his apartment and shot him dead. She said she thought she was entering her own apartment and that Jean was an intruder. In 2019 Elijah McClain, accused of no more than being "sketchy," was knocked to the ground by three police officers in Aurora, Colorado. One officer held him to the ground, cuffed his hands behind his back, and injected him with ketamine to forcibly sedate him. McClain went into cardiac arrest and died three days later in hospital. The same year Atatiana Jefferson was shot and killed in her home in Fort Worth, Texas, by a police officer. The police were called by a neighbor, who had simply reported that Jefferson's front door was open.

Black people were killed in their backyards, eating ice cream in their living rooms, sleeping in their bedrooms, standing in their grandparents' house, on their lawns, and outside their homes. Many of these violent deaths started as everyday police interactions. Law professor Devon Carbado writes about how ordinary front-end encounters, such as routine traffic stops or welfare checks, when compressed through a racialized policing system, can lead more easily and quickly to back-end violence by police on Black motorists and householders. Black people are much more vulnerable to police violence, not just in highly charged situations, but also in the context of everyday encounters.[33]

Just two months before Floyd's death in Minneapolis, Breonna Taylor was killed in her own home in Louisville, Kentucky, when three police officers entered her apartment under a no-knock warrant. Taylor's boyfriend, imagining that they were experiencing a home invasion, fired a warning shot. The three officers fired 32 rounds and Taylor died after six of the bullets entered her body. By the time that the haunting images circulated of Chauvin's featureless expression as he pressed his full weight onto Floyd's neck, there was already an organizational base, simmering community anger, and social mobilization against police violence, and a long overdue debate about race and racism had been ignited.

The image of Chauvin's knee on Floyd's neck was a searing indictment of racism. For many there was recognition that the legacy of slavery and racism is all around us. In the United States, there were demonstrations around statues of slavers, racists, and their apologists and enablers. The naming of u.s. military establishments after Southern Civil War generals was criticized. In the National Football League (NFL), the Washington football team changed its name, after years of unavailing protest, from the Washington Redskins to the Commanders. Across the country, there was a racial reckoning that called into question all those myths and legends as well as practices that were part of the continuing racist legacy. Statues were toppled and vandalized. Streets and buildings were renamed. In June 2020, a county board in Virginia voted to rename Lee Highway for John Langston, the first Black man elected to Congress from Virginia. The racial reckoning was global as much as national. That same month, June 2020, in Bristol, England, where I went to graduate school, the statue of Edward Colston (1636–1721), a wealthy slaver and city philanthropist, was prized off its pediment, rolled down the street, and dumped unceremoniously into the river Avon.

In America, there were calls for police reform.[34] There was a vigorous debate about how to improve policing to fix the problems of rogue cops, poor training, weak oversight, and pervasive racism among departments. Many specific ideas were floated, including:

Banning use of chemical irritants and chokeholds
Banning no-knock warrants
Nonviolent means of defusing situations
Not hiring police officers with a history of violence
    and using better background checks

Wresting sole control of disciplining of police from police
officials

Redirecting police spending away from traditional policing

Reducing the militarization of police

Greater transparency and swifter accountability of police
actions, especially violent ones

Greater use and enforcement of body cameras for all police
officers.

More specific suggestions included strengthening internal
accounting so that police departments themselves rather than
jurisdictions pay civil costs of actions, to give an incentive to identify and eject bad actors in the force; preventing violent officers
from keeping their jobs or moving to new ones (one-quarter of all
officers fired for misconduct get their jobs back); and weakening
the immunity of police so that they are not separated from the
legal consequences of their actions.[35] There was also an acceptance of the difficulties of the job, with proposals to reduce police
workloads, increase pay, and provide better training and working
conditions.

There are major obstacles to police reform. Police unions are
very powerful in local communities and resist any form of dis-
ciplinary proceedings outside of police control. There is such an
intense loyalty in the bunker-like mentality of police departments
that it is difficult to break a code of silence over bad behaviors.
Police reform often runs up against the entrenched power of those
veteran officers unwilling to change.[36]

A Long Hot Summer

There were demonstrations in the streets. The organization Black Lives Matter (BLM) was formed in 2013 in response to the mounting images of police violence, its very name a reminder that racial inequality in policing could be deadly. BLM was a major force, but not the only one, behind the mobilization of at least 15 million people in the summer and early fall of 2020. In June 2020 at least two-thirds of adult Americans expressed some support for the movement's goal of criminal justice reform.[37] BLM organized demonstrations in over 2,000 locations in the United States that summer. Most were peaceful, but violence did occur, including rioting, vandalism and arson.

Throughout the summer of 2020 there were protests and counterprotests in cities and towns across the country. In some cases, when statues were threatened with destruction or demolition by activists or town councils, right-wing militias in full battle dress and guns came out in force. Protests were met with counterprotests. In late August 2020 in Kenosha, Wisconsin, a satellite city about an hour's drive from both Milwaukee and Chicago, protests and civil unrest followed the non-fatal shooting of a Black man, Jacob Blake, by a White police officer. On August 25, "patriots" came to Kenosha in response to a call to take up arms and defend the city. Militia groups posted solicitations for people to come armed. The call attracted men who had been present at other protests in Wisconsin that summer. A seventeen-year-old, Kyle Rittenhouse, came armed with a semi-automatic AR15-style rifle. On the night of August 25, he shot and killed two men and wounded a third. After Rittenhouse shot the first man four times at close range, a crowd pursued him and when one man struck him with a skateboard, Rittenhouse fatally shot him in the chest. Another man, armed with a handgun, was shot in the right arm by Rittenhouse and survived. Rittenhouse had participated in local police cadet programs and had expressed support for Blue Lives Matter, a pro-police movement that grew as a direct counterresponse to the BLM movement. At his trial Rittenhouse claimed that he took his rifle with him to Kenosha to help defend small business owners. He was found not guilty in a unanimous verdict.

The long hot summer of 2020 witnessed peaceful protest, violent confrontations, and occasional rioting in various places, but things were especially tense in the nation's capital. In June, a large military presence of national guardsmen from around the country was deployed on the steps of the Lincoln Memorial. There were police barricades around the statue of Abraham Lincoln in the namesake park in Capitol Hill, just twelve blocks from the Capitol. The Emancipation Memorial statue in the middle of the park depicts a standing Lincoln beside a kneeling Black man. The iconography was problematic at the best of times, and these were not the best of times. Further west in the city, after nights of demonstrations, vandalism, and arson, downtown Washington was heavily policed by federal and city forces. The White House was cordoned off with fencing and guarded by armed personnel from various federal agencies including the Federal Prison Service, Homeland Security, and National Park Police. Trump stewed and fretted, especially after a rumor circulated that he had been evacuated to the president's secret basement bunker. The security perimeter around the White House was extended to include Lafayette Square. Demonstrators massed at the edge of the Square outside the fence at 16th Street Northwest. On

June 1, 2020, police officers on horseback and others in full riot gear cleared protestors from the area using flash grenades, tear gas, and rubber bullets. At the time, there was no violence among the protestors. Later, police said that they issued a warning but no one in the crowd—bystanders, demonstrators, or reporters— heard any such warning. It was an engineered media opportunity for Trump, who was flanked by members of his family and his cabinet, which included attorney general Barr, the defense secretary Mark Esper, and chief of staff Mark Meadows. The group also included General Milley, chairman of the Joint Chiefs of Staff, the nation's highest ranking u.s. military office, who was dressed in combat fatigues. They walked through the cleared space to the two-hundred-year-old St John's Episcopal Church. At the entrance, Trump held up a Bible. He stood awkwardly, unsure how to handle the sacred book. As he stood self-consciously and stiffly, reporters asked if it was his Bible. Trump, who played golf rather than attended church on Sundays, replied, "It's a Bible." It was a made-for-evangelical-television moment: Trump ordering a space to be cleared of peaceful protestors so that he could brandish the Bible. Later that evening, the aggressive tactics continued when a military helicopter flew to rooftop level in Chinatown to intimidate fleeing civilians.

The event is important for many reasons. To some extent it was a success for Trump. He changed the narrative; he was no longer a coward cowering in a bunker, but the strong, resolute, and religious leader of America. It also helped to shift the wider narrative from racial injustice to law and order. His base responded enthusiastically to the clearing of demonstrators and the invocation of religion. But it came at a cost. It rallied Trump's critics, who noted that armed police essentially squashed a peaceful expression of First Amendment rights so that the president could stage an obviously manufactured media event. A few days later, the mayor of Washington, DC, Muriel Bowser, had two blocks of 16th Street Northwest running north from Lafayette Square renamed Black Lives Matter Plaza and painted in giant yellow letters reading Black Lives Matter. The signage was to become a constant image in subsequent television reporting. The event also alienated some of the military leadership. General Milley was appalled and embarrassed that he was used as a prop in such a blatant piece of propaganda and claimed later that he believed he was only accompanying Trump to review the National Guard outside Lafayette Square. He let it be known that he was against the use of military force to quell peaceful civil protest. The use of military helicopters in the streets of DC was also widely criticized. This was DC and not Fallujah, after all. The top military brass felt used by Trump and wanted no repeat of the bad optics of overwhelming military force against domestic protestors. Better public relations demanded a less visible military presence. It was agreed that peaceful protests should not be met again with such force. Remember this decision when we examine the events of January 6.

The Second Crisis of Policing

Throughout the summer of 2020, city streets were filled with police and protestors, statues were vandalized, arson and theft were committed. The country was at its most fractious. Unrest was directly triggered by the experience and responses to COVID-19, as well as the racial justice protest in the wake of George Floyd's death. One study counted 1,054 incidents in New York, 459 in Portland, and

428 in Los Angeles.[38] Portland stands out. With a population of little more than half a million, it had more civil disturbances than Los Angeles, which has a metro population of roughly 12.5 million. The city was a hotbed of civil unrest; it had a well-organized anti-racism movement as well as a history of previous social mobilizations and anti-Trump demonstrations.

In Minneapolis, the epicenter of the policing crisis, escalating violence and vandalism were fueled by rage and poor crisis management. A report commissioned by the city found poor communications and failures of leadership by senior politicians and officials. The police failed to follow consistent rules of engagement, and those on the frontline operated without supervision or restraint. Police fired tear gas, rubber bullets, and chemical munitions into crowds of protestors, often without first calling for the crowd to disperse. At least 45 people were seriously injured and sixteen suffered traumatic brain injuries; one man was blinded in one eye after he was hit with a rubber bullet. The police aggression helped to fuel even more violence and did little to stop looting.[39]

The poor policing in Minneapolis was replicated in cities across the United States. In 2020 in Denver, police employed indiscriminate and excessive force on protestors. Later, demonstrators were awarded $14 million in court, as police were found to have violated their constitutional rights. Authorities are settling similar lawsuits in Austin, New York City, and Richmond. There are ongoing criminal cases against police in Dallas. Findings from other cities all report police forces were ill-prepared, poorly equipped, and inadequately trained to deal with peaceful demonstrations. In many cases there was the use of excessive force and an obvious failure to distinguish between peaceful demonstrators and troublemakers.[40]

The initial crisis of policing was the reality of persistent violence against Black people. The response to this crisis included protests, attempts at reconciliation, a renewed discussion about policing, and a wider and deeper racial reckoning. But there was a second crisis of policing. This lay in the perception in the minds of many Americans that the forces of disorder were undermining society. These Americans responded not to the images of police violence but to the images of protestors on the streets and riots in the city. The crisis of policing to them meant the perceived breakdown of law and order. This other crisis of policing had a basis in fact. There were scenes of disorder and violence, looting and arson. For an older generation it seemed like a return to the anarchy and mayhem of the 1960s and '70s. This crisis was hyped by Trump, his allies, and the Trump-friendly media, especially Fox News. They were successful, at least with some of the u.s. public, in shifting the narrative away from racial justice and police misconduct to law and order. There was of course a racial tinge to the pivot. For some, blm was a call for racial justice, but for others it was a menace to society. An alternative narrative blamed the unrest on liberal Democrats who were soft on crime—a reliable and often-used trope in the Republican playbook—and shadowy groups such as antifa.

Antifa is more of an ideology than an organization, so it is difficult to assess its actual numbers and its activities. What is crystal clear, however, is that it became a great talking point for Trump, who fed the narrative of shadowy, dangerous groups working to destroy society with embroidered tales of people dressed all in black traveling around the country causing mayhem. Antifa's loosely organized and at times ephemeral presence allowed it to become a spectral force in the conservative imagination as the source of disorder, and the cause of unrest. Trump argued that he was what stood between the silent White majority and young, black-clad anarchists out to destroy society. Antifa rented more room in Trump's head than they occupied in the real world. This is not to say there were not anarchist groups at work behind some of the violent scenes in city streets in the summer of 2020, but their influence was magnified to bolster Trump's electioneering agenda. Talking about antifa and about violence against police officers shifted attention away from the unfolding public health crisis and the enduring problem of racial inequality. The free-floating anxiety caused by the continuing pandemic, and economic uncertainty and growing precarity, could land on the comforting cushion of a tried and tested law-and-order narrative. The position was reinforced by some of the discourses on police reforms. The term "defunding the police" was a gift to Trump and his supporters. They interpreted it as a brazen attempt by liberals who wanted to abolish policing in all its forms in order to undermine society. Images of unpoliced cities overrun by violent criminals and anarchists were soon touted. In reality, the call to defund the police had a basis in reform debates. One proposal was to shift resources away from aggressive warrior-style policing to mental health professionals and to adopt more crime reduction and prevention programs. The subtleties were lost as the debate heated up. Trump and his supporters worked to turn the narrative away from racial injustice toward law and order.

There was also a cultural fallout. The racial reckoning provoked a backlash. The countermovement latched onto an academic discourse known as "critical race theory," an attempt to uncover the racialized nature of u.s. society. The theory informed the 1619 Project, a journalistic initiative which sought to establish a new origin story for the United States based on racial subjugation, linking back to when the first Black slaves were brought to the colonies.[41] Conservative commentators, as well as parents and school administrators influenced by right-wing oratory, would see in critical race theory an attempt to demonize the United States, by making all White people the villains of America rather than its God-ordained saviours, thus disturbing their illusion of a race-neutral society. The term became shorthand for the idea that the people espousing it were critics of the United States whose sole goal was to weaken society and tear down the comforts of White America. It was the manufacturing of outrage to counter a long-delayed racial reckoning. The reaction to critical race theory was to take center stage in 2021 and especially in 2022. After the events of January 6, it was a way for the conservative right wing to hang onto some semblance of relevance as the Trump brand lost its value with the general public in the wake of the insurrection.

The pandemic created bad press for Trump but activated his extreme right-wing support. The initial crisis of policing began with a disturbing video of a police officer killing a man for a petty crime; this initiated a racial reckoning, but in turn the outrage shown against police and government led to images of street protest and violence being used, in the second crisis of policing, by Trump and his supporters. If the pandemic revealed Trump's incompetence, the urban unrest gave him an opportunity to pose as a strong figure in a time of disorder. In October 2020 he refused to condemn White supremacists and hate groups, and tweeted,

Biden and Democrats refuse to condemn Antifa, Anarchists, Looters and Mobs that burn down Democrat run cities.

This second crisis of policing was not the usual law-and-order narrative. There was a more strident, interventionist rhetoric. There was open talk of employing the 1807 Insurrection Act, legislation that would have given the president very broad powers to deploy federal troops. After the summer of 2020 Trump continued to suggest invoking the 1807 Act to deploy active-duty troops across the country to quell protests. Some of Trump's civilian advisors ramped up the rhetoric. The defense secretary, Mark Esper, spoke about the need to control the "battle space," by which he meant the streets of American cities. The attorney general, William Barr, argued for the need to "dominate the streets." Trump wanted General Milley to crack down with armed troops. At one point Trump asked for 10,000 active-duty troops to be deployed. Senior military brass, and even Esper and Barr, resisted Trump's demand.[42] But the Insurrection Act had entered the White House conversations and Trump's thinking. It was not a huge step from talking about the need to invoke the Act to deal with social protests to later conflating an unfavorable election result with the need for an active military intervention.

6

The Coup

If we define an insurrection as an attempt to undermine the results of a legitimate election, there were, in fact, two insurrections. The first was the attempted coup by the president, his allies, and senior Republicans to effectively annul the results of the 2020 presidential election through dubious legal challenges, attempted vote tampering, and the fraudulent use of fake electors. Unable to change the outcome of the election, despite his best efforts, Trump and his allies then mobilized supporters to physically contest the confirmation of Biden as president. This second insurrection was the more widely known assault on the Capitol on January 6, 2021. Attention has naturally focused on this second event. In this chapter, I will look at the first insurrection, best described as an attempted coup—one that, if it had come to pass, would have destroyed democracy in the USA.

The Election

In the hyperpartisan money-driven circus that is electioneering in the United States, there are few quiet times. The notion of an election cycle assumes an oscillation between quiet and then hectic periods. A more appropriate image might be a stove that is always hot but at certain times becomes incandescent. The year of a presidential election, which comes around every four years, is particularly incendiary since not only the presidency is at stake but often control of the House and the Senate. Presidential election years pull in more voters and attract more media attention than other election periods. Average turnout is only around 40 percent of the eligible voters in midterms but closer to 60 percent in presidential election years. Despite the challenge of the COVID-19 pandemic, the 2020 election had the highest turnout of any U.S. presidential election in the twenty-first century. In total, 17 million more people, 5 percentage points more, voted in 2020 compared to in 2016. The high turnout, at least for the United States, of 67 percent of all eligible voters was indicative of the passions generated in this election.[1]

The months leading up to the election were traumatic. There was the pandemic and then the social unrest in the wake of the death of George Floyd on May 25, 2020. The rising body count from COVID-19, the pandemic disruption to normal life, and the searing images of police violence and social unrest unsettled the nation. A very polarized electorate added to the tension. Trump's bedrock support not only held firm but became ever more convinced of the existential necessity of his victory. His opponents meanwhile saw a Trump second term as a clear and present danger to the Republic. They saw the last year of his presidency as one in which he was so concerned with reelection that he played down the COVID threat and pushed to keep the economy open—resulting in needless deaths—and promoted narratives that tore at the coherence of the Republic. With so much at stake, few elections in recent history have had such a toxic mix of apprehension and passion. It was a highly personalized election because the defining issue was Donald Trump. The Republican Party had become the party of Trump. In previous years, the party's policy document, announced at the party convention, had outlined a detailed agenda. In 2020, in striking contrast, the party produced just a one-page document for its platform. The official document simply asserted that the party "enthusiastically supports President Trump and continues to reject the policy positions of the Obama Biden administration."[2] In other words, the party would back anything Trump proposed; it had no other policies, and had given up any pretense of announcing otherwise or enacting legislation. Republicans were now bound to the fate of Trump's election success or failure. The election was, for all intents and purposes, a referendum on Donald Trump.

The election of 2020 was held in the shadow of the pandemic. Early voting with mail-in ballots was encouraged in order to avoid transmission of the virus, with many states making it easier to do so as well as allowing those votes to come in earlier than usual. However, Republicans and Trump had long resisted early voting and mail-in ballots as they were widely believed to favor Democratic voters. Republican officials prioritized Election Day voting over postal ballots.

The greater use of early mail-in voting made the counting of votes more complex and drawn out. Even in the best of years there is an issue with counting votes in the United States. Elections in America are a haphazard thing, administered by individual states and reliant on a multitude of paid and unpaid officials and volunteers spread out across a patchwork of myriad administrative units. This politicized, part-time, and widely dispersed system can and sometimes does create disparities and uncertainty in how votes are counted and recorded. And because responsibility is so widely diffused, elections can more easily be influenced by local interests. In 2020, officials in key states such as Arizona and Georgia had to respond to false claims of election fraud as activists harassed election workers. The counts went on despite a deluge of mail-in ballots and attempts by Republican lawmakers to make voting harder. In Erie, Pennsylvania, right-wing activists accused the local postmaster of election fraud. He was hounded on social media and received death threats.

Even in normal years, a cumbersome process means a long time passes from the final election result to the inauguration of the elected president. The election takes place on the first Tuesday in November, but the inauguration does not take place until January 20 of the following year.[3] As we now know, this inordinately long time for a defeated president to still effectively oversee the power of the state, at least six weeks, is not necessarily a good thing. Especially if the sitting president and many of his supporters believe his victory has been stolen.

In the 2020 election more than 158 million votes were cast— 100 million of them by early mail-in voting. Biden won. And he won big. Biden and his vice-presidential candidate Kamala Harris received 81 million votes. Trump and Mike Pence received 74 million votes. Compared to 2016, there was a modest decline in Trump's base support. The Republican advantage among White men without a college degree declined from 48 percent to 42 percent. The decrease in Republican support was even more pronounced for 45–64-year-old White Americans, whose level of support for Trump declined from 28 percent in 2016 to 19 percent in 2020. Biden had a clear advantage with young voters, college educated voters, and women voters. And crucially, Trump's defeat was due to the erosion of his support in key battleground states

such as Pennsylvania, Michigan, and Wisconsin. It was the culmination of a year of incompetent governance and growing fears
of a second Trump term. The result epitomized Trump's presidential career. He could mobilize his core support but could not
extend his appeal.

Biden won most of the mail-in voters. However, on election
night, the first votes recorded in many states were those of voters
who cast their ballots in person, and the results leaned Republican.
Very soon after the polls closed the early results in vital states such
as Arizona and Georgia gave the advantage to Trump, but as
the hours passed and the mail-in votes were counted, the victory
shifted Biden's way. The more ballots that were counted, the more
Trump's lead was first cut, then overturned. But his early "winning" became fixed in his brain and subsequently he could never
believe anything else.

The Big Lie

Losing is never easy. Rather than admitting you did something
wrong, like having a failed strategy or incompetent tactics, it is
always much easier to blame your opponent. Or the system.

Trump had a long history of claiming fraud. Ever fearful of
being considered a loser, Trump had long employed the tactic of
signaling unfair elections in advance. If he lost, he didn't really
lose since the result was fixed. If he won, that made his victory even more impressive as he had had to overcome an unfair
system. He used this tactic in the 2016 primaries, when at a rally
in Columbus, Ohio, on August 1, he said, "the primary season
was rigged and I'm afraid the election is going to be rigged, I have
to be honest."

He claimed fraud even when he won. In the 2016 presidential election, Trump won the presidency because he gained more Electoral College votes than Hillary Clinton (304 to 227). But he lost the popular vote. Trump garnered 62.9 million votes while Clinton received 65.8 million. Trump was so incensed that he claimed millions of "illegal" immigrants had voted. In May 2017 he even established an Advisory Committee on Election Integrity to review claims of vote fraud. The commission was abandoned in January 2018 after no evidence was revealed, several original members had resigned in disgust at its overt partisanship, and eight lawsuits were filed against its impartiality. Even as he dissolved the commission, Trump continued to claim voter fraud, all in an election where he ostensibly had won the presidency. So, it should have come as no big surprise that he reacted the way he did when he *actually* lost the presidency.

Trump had sown distrust in the democratic process for months, raising doubts about the election as early as the spring of 2020 as polls both public and private showed that he could lose. He complained of voter registration irregularities and sowed the seeds of doubt about the veracity of the outcome:

> *millions of mail in ballots will be printed by foreign countries*
> *and others it will be the scandal of our times*
> Trump tweet on June 22, 2020

> *I think mail involved voting is going to rig the election*
> Interview on Fox News, July 19, 2020

The disruptive claim was widely believed among the wealthy donor base of the Republican right. Stephen Hotze was a GOP donor who funded a group, Liberty Center for God and Country, that was searching for voter fraud even before the election. Hotze believed the wild fantasy that undocumented Hispanic children were being used to forge three-quarters of a million phony ballots to rig the election in Harris County, Texas. He hired private investigators to follow a white van he believed was transporting phony ballots to be used in the upcoming election. He even invited the federal prosecutor in Texas to arrest the van's driver. With no official action forthcoming, a private investigator employed by Hotze ran the white van off the road and held the driver at gunpoint. No forged ballots were ever found. The driver was an air-conditioning repairman; the truck was carrying repair parts.[4]

Trump had established the narrative of the Big Lie in the months before the election, ramped up the rhetoric as the election drew closer, and turned it up to full blast after the results were announced. Within hours of the defeat, he and his allies started to make the claim that he did not lose the election, it was stolen. They said there was widespread fraud and so the election result was illegitimate. In tweets and announcements, he discredited the declared result for Biden, stating that "Radical Left democrats" had stolen the election.[5] He claimed, without any proof, that he had garnered millions more votes than his rival and that a conspiracy of people across the country had worked to undermine his election victory. He refused to concede defeat.

The narrative was also commodified. Many wealthy Republicans funded campaigns to overturn the election. The financier Fredric Eshelman, for example, donated $2.5 million to a group that claimed it was undertaking a voter fraud investigation. As it turned out, the organization, True the Vote, was also an opportunity for its directors to use the funds for self-enrichment and backhand deals. Eshelman took the group to court to try to get his money back but lost the case. True the Vote was just one of many organizations that had aggressively promoted claims of voter fraud and pushed for voter identification laws in the lead-up to the election. The group quickly pivoted to fundraising to contest the result of the 2020 election through federal lawsuits in Georgia, Michigan, Pennsylvania, and Wisconsin. True the Vote, like other organizations, raised lots of money on the backs of the claims of a rigged election.

The Coup Attempt

After the loss, numerous close advisors to Trump argued, to account for his unwillingness to concede defeat, that he just needed time and space to process the results. They believed that he would eventually come round to the inevitable conclusion that he lost the election and join the long tradition in American politics of the loser accepting defeat. He never did. He was always guided by the existential need to always be seen as a winner. No one stood up to him, so the "space" given by his advisors, toadies, and colleagues, such as the always subservient vice president Mike Pence, to recover from the defeat, was immediately filled with advisors peddling conspiracy theories. Rudy Giuliani, the former mayor of New York City and now a Trump confidante, and Sidney Powell, a firm believer in the wackiest of conspiracy theories, took on more central positions.

The coup had two parts. First was the claim of fraud. From the election results until January 11, there was the constant assertion that the result was false. Giuliani counseled Trump to just say, "we won." The phrase "Frankly we did win this election" was used to set the tone for the next eleven weeks. Rudy Giuliani took the lead in alleging the hacking of voting machines and outright fraud and became the main fraud-whisperer constantly repeating the message that the election was stolen, and that Trump was the rightful winner.[6] This first part of the coup was to undermine the democratic process by claiming with no real proof that the election result was fraudulent. The sitting president and his cronies led the charge to undermine trust and confidence in the electoral process, delegitimize the incoming administration, and seriously compromise American democracy.

The second part of the coup was the attempt to overturn the results. Trump's chief of staff, Mark Meadows, who had cast doubt on the election even before the result, forwarded claims of a conspiracy theory involving Italian technology and shadowy foreign agents. He was in close contact with Supreme Court Justice Clarence Thomas's wife, Virginia (Ginny), who repeated wild conspiracy theories and urged the overturning of Biden's victory.[7] Meadows played an outsized role as he tried to influence vote counting in Georgia, lobbied the DOJ, and suggested that Vice President Pence reject electoral votes. As Trump's point man, and with all the authority of the White House, he actively worked to overturn the results of the legitimate election, to keep his boss and presumably himself in power.[8] And in a story that reeks of bitter irony, while pushing the claims of voting fraud by his political opponents, he actually committed it himself when he falsely claimed, in applying for an absentee ballot, that his residence was a mobile home in North Carolina, a place that he did not own and had never lived in.[9] It is impossible to make this stuff up.

Joe Biden won the presidential election because he won a majority of votes in the Electoral College. In the second part of the coup, Trump, his key supporters, and Republican operatives sought to overturn this majority in a series of moves that would give the victory to Trump. One plan hatched immediately after the election by Rudy Giuliani and other co-conspiracists was to disrupt the Electoral College process.

Some background: Before the election, presidential candidates or their parties in each state nominate electors. In most cases there are slates of Republican and Democratic electors. After the counting of the popular vote in a state, the governor certifies the electors of the winning candidate and they then meet in mid-December to record their votes and send the certificates to a joint session of Congress chaired by the vice president. These certificates are tallied on January 6 in a ceremonial event in the Congress.

One of Trump's lawyers, John Eastman, argued that Pence did not need to recognize the Electoral College votes for Biden. On November 28, Eastman wrote a seven-page memo, "The Constitutional Authority of State Legislatures to Choose Electors," where he outlined a scheme to present fake electors. In the confusion, Pence would then have a reason to overturn the election at the January 6 ceremony. It had no legal basis, as Eastman well knew. A u.s. District Judge, David O. Carter, said it was a coup in search of a legal theory. On December 14, 2020, "fake" Republican electors convened in the capitals of five states—Arizona, Georgia, Michigan, Nevada, and Wisconsin—that Joe Biden had won. These fake electors declared themselves "duly elected and qualified," then sent signed certificates to Washington purporting to affirm Donald Trump as the actual victor. By submitting an alternative slate of electors, the conspirators hoped to provide constitutional authority for the vice president to reject or delay counting the legitimate electoral votes. Overturning the votes of these five states would be enough to swing the vote in Trump's favor. The vice president's legal team did not believe that there was a legal basis and several Republicans who were original Trump electors did not go along with the scheme.[10] However, the pressure persisted. On January 4, 2021, Eastman spoke to Pence about overturning the election results by either rejecting the electoral count or suspending the day's proceedings and sending back a new round of vote counting to seven states. Trump persisted with the idea that the vice president had the power to overturn the results.

There was also a campaign to press Republican elected officials in key states such as Georgia and Arizona to take back the electoral votes for Biden and hand them instead to Trump. The Georgia secretary of state, Brad Raffensperger, and the speaker of the Arizona House of Representatives, Rusty Bowers, received calls from Trump and Giuliani asking them to put forward the illegitimate pro-Trump electors. Raffensperger was also told to find extra votes to ensure a Trump majority in the state. Bowers received pressure from the White House right up to the morning of January 6. GOP officials including Michigan State Senate majority leader Mike Shirkey and Pennsylvania House speaker Bryan Cutler also received calls from Team Trump to overturn the results.

There was also the use of questionable legal strategies. Questionable, because Trump was told by the more legitimate legal advisors that there was little evidence of fraud. He was told not long after the polls closed that he was going to lose the election. Top officials at the DOJ told him repeatedly that the allegations of fraud were unfounded. In his memoir, former attorney general William Barr records that he told Trump in a meeting in the Oval Office on December 1 that the claims of fraud had no basis in fact. Despite this advice, the DOJ was bombarded with requests from the White House to pursue the stolen election narrative in legal challenges to the Supreme Court and to the states. The DOJ declined, and even Barr, a resolute Trump supporter until then, refused to go along with Trump's story. He was replaced on December 14 with the second-in-command at the DOJ, Jeffrey Rosen. Trump wrote to Rosen even before the latter had taken up the position, asking him to embrace the theory of voter fraud. Rosen was called to Trump's office on December 15 and told to file legal briefs authorizing lawsuits to overturn the election results. Rosen refused, telling the president that the DOJ had found no evidence of fraud. The acting deputy attorney general Richard Donoghue told Trump on a phone call on December 27, 2020, that the major allegations were not supported by the evidence.[11] Trump persisted with the Big Lie. Rosen's unwillingness to go along with the legal conspiracy almost got him fired on January 3. On New Year's Eve, Trump considered replacing Rosen with Jeffrey Bossert Clark, who was more than willing to promote the voter fraud conspiracy and to force state lawmakers to overturn the November results in the states narrowly won by Biden. Only the very real threat of mass resignations by senior officials in the DOJ made Trump keep Rosen in place.

The coup involved electoral intimidation. Across the country election officials were harassed. Dubious legal challenges were also mounted. Two journalists, Mark Bowden and Matthew Teague, collected evidence from six key states. From late October to late December 2020, eight lawsuits claiming electoral fraud were filed in Arizona, eight in Georgia, seven in Michigan, nine in Pennsylvania, and six in Wisconsin. All the cases were either dismissed or denied.[12]

Seventeen Republican state attorney generals filed a lawsuit on December 7 to overturn the result in four states. It was spurious since it was filed in Texas and sought to overturn voter results of other states. Many of the 26 Republican politicians who signed up for this campaign were lawyers and should have known better, but their support was meant to curry favor with Trump and to feed resentment in the populist base.

There were also direct attempts to maintain Trump's presidency by senior Republican figures, such as Senator Ted Cruz, of Texas, who hatched a plan to formally object in the Senate on January 6 to the results in six swing states, ask for a ten-day audit, and effectively turn the decision back to GOP state legislatures, who would most likely overturn the results. Ten other senators backed this proposal.[13] Another Republican senator, Mike Lee of Utah, promoted spurious legal challenges and lobbied state lawmakers to find a justification not to count the electoral votes for Biden.[14]

More dramatic plans were hatched by those at the crazier edges of the Trump court. One memo produced in December 2020 suggested that Trump should use the National Security Agency and Defense Department to sift through raw electronic communications to show that foreign powers had intervened in the 2020 election. The draft of an executive order was circulated proposing the seizure of voting machines. At a White House meeting on December 14, Trump talked of military intervention and of more appeals to the Supreme Court. On December 18, at a meeting in the Oval Office with his national security advisor and leading conspiracy supporter Michael Flynn, the talk was of deploying the military to overturn the 2020 election and of a federal seizure of voting machines. A meeting was held on January 4 at Trump International Hotel attended by at least three Republican senators who had heard allegations that the 2020 election had been influenced by foreign powers and that voting machines needed to be investigated, especially in those states that Trump had expected to win but lost. Michael Flynn advocated using the military to organize a rerun of the election in so-called battleground states.[15]

There was wider resistance to accepting the results of the election. From November 3, 2020, to the Electoral College vote on January 6, 2021, Trump and the Republican National Committee were raising almost $3 million every day online. "We will have civil war in the streets before Biden will be prez," was just one of the many thousands of quotes on the Internet that called for a silent majority to demand that battleground states not certify fraudulent elections. Between Election Day and January 6, a steady rate of 10,000 posts a day on average attacked the election results as fraudulent and demanded that true patriots stand up for their country and defeat the liberal threat.[16]

The Insurrection Act was also invoked to undermine the election of Biden. The Act, first introduced in 1807, was last used in 1992 in the wake of urban rioting after the police who assaulted Rodney King were found not guilty. The possibility was first raised in the spring of 2020 by Trump and some conservatives to subdue the social justice protests. Republican Senator Tom Cotton wrote a *New York Times* opinion piece urging the law's use.[17] By the end of the year it was seen as a possible tactic to keep Trump in power. The leader of the Oath Keepers, Stewart Rhodes, argued that the Insurrection Act could and should be used by Trump to declare a national emergency. He outlined his plan with arch conspiracy theorist Alex Jones on a program broadcast on Infowars on November 9, 2020. Rhodes urged Trump to use the Act to suppress the "deep state." The more extreme conspiracists hoped that the Act could be used to keep Trump in power.

Despite such frantic activity, things were moving against Trump. On December 14, the Electoral College confirmed Biden's victory. The process was heading inexorably to the joint session of Congress on January 6. As the day approached, Trump became more desperate. He continued to publicly claim a fraudulent election, press the DOJ, and lobby state officials. On January 2 he called the Georgia secretary of state, Raffensperger, asking him to "find" enough votes to overturn the Democratic victory. The same day a phone meeting was held between Trump allies and three hundred state legislators presumably to coordinate a plan to overturn Biden's electoral votes. On January 3, Clark told associates he was going to replace Rosen at the DOJ. He drew up a plan to overhaul the leadership of federal law enforcement in the days leading up to January 6.

By early January, the legal challenges had wilted in the clear light of judicial review. Plans to invoke the Insurrection Act and employ the military all evaporated. Senior military personnel were wary of being dragged into the political morass. Now the only thing standing between Trump and outright defeat was the January 6 congressional confirmation. His legal advisors told him that his best hope was to persuade the vice president, who traditionally presided over the ceremony, to overturn the result. After all the legal challenges and White House pressure on state officials had failed to change the results, Trump came to believe that his best remaining hope to cling to unelected power was for Pence to overturn the result. And to make that happen he organized a rally.

7

The Assault on the Capitol

The Electoral Count Act of 1887 states that at 1 p.m. on January 6, following a presidential election, the House and Senate will meet in a joint session, over which the president of the Senate will preside. The electoral votes from the fifty states and the District of Columbia will then be opened and counted.

This singular moment in American democracy is the only official declaration announcing the winner of the presidential election. It is a ceremonial event, a symbolic certification, usually chaired by the vice president. It is normally considered a formality. But after their political coup failed, Trump and his associates sought to use the event to undermine the democratic process. It was their third attempt, after the Big Lie and the political coup, to overturn the results.

The Rally

Between Election Day on November 3, 2020, and January 6, 2021, at a steady rate of 10,000 a day, on average, Facebook and other social media posts attacked the election results as fraudulent and called on true patriots to stand up, save the country and "mobilize against the corrupt communist Marxist scummy democrats."[1]

On December 19, Trump tweeted,

Statistically impossible to have lost the 2020 election. Big protest in DC on January 6th. Be there will be wild.

His Big Lie was endorsed and amplified by Republican representatives such as Jim Jordan, who also encouraged attendance at the rally. Event organizers included the conspiracist Michael Flynn as well as Trump loyalists such as Katrina Pierson and Steve Bannon. The rally was also promoted by a variety of right-wing groups, including the Tea Party Patriots and Republican Attorneys General Association—the principal law officers in the individual states—and the Council for National Policy (CNP), a secretive group of conservative Christian activists. A year before, Pence had sent a letter to the CNP thanking them for "consistently amplifying the agenda of President Trump." One CNP member, Ali Alexander, who started the #StoptheSteal website, led protests the day before the big rally with chants of "Victory or Death." He also discussed security arrangements with two extremist groups, the Proud Boys and Oath Keepers.

Thousands followed the call to come to DC. There was even a crowdfunding website, givesendgo, with a request "to sponsor a warrior." There are no accurate figures for the actual numbers who eventually turned up, only estimates, but the likelihood is between 10,000 and 20,000.

On January 3, an intelligence report by the Capitol police warned of a violent scenario for the forthcoming march. It noted that the president's backers' desperation and disappointment could lead to violence. The next day, Pentagon officials informed the mayor of Washington, DC, Muriel Bowser, that the

National Guard would be activated but with significant restrictions. Mindful of the bad press received earlier in the summer of 2020, the officials ordered that no Humvees or other militarized vehicles would be used. The National Park Service increased the expected number of participants to 30,000.

On January 5, amid growing concerns about the swelling numbers of expected protestors, Bowser sent letters to the acting attorney general, the army secretary, and the acting defense secretary about the need for a federal law enforcement presence. At 4 p.m. the congressman in charge of the financial oversight of Capitol police, Representative Tim Ryan of Ohio, held a conference with the Capitol police chief and other security officials. He was assured that every precaution was being taken.

On the morning of January 6, the wife of Supreme Court Justice Clarence Thomas, Virginia Thomas, tweeted *"LOVE MAGA people!!!!"*[2] She was a regular communicator with her 10,000-person chatroom, where she repeated an old lie oft-spouted by the extreme right wing, that the Holocaust was caused by Germany's gun control laws. She shared links about supposed corruption by Joe Biden and his son. She repeated QAnon-inspired conspiracies. It will come as no surprise that her husband is one of the more conservative justices on a Supreme Court now packed with right-wing partisans. She praised the rushed confirmation in 2020 of the Trump nominee Amy Coney Barrett as "a day President Trump made possible." Emails were later discovered between her and Mark Meadows, then Trump's chief of staff, which repeated and affirmed the conspiracy-inspired narrative of the need to overthrow the results of the election. Not all MAGA supporters and conspiracists live on the margins of u.s. society.

At 7 a.m. on the morning of January 6, 2021, the chief of the Capitol Police called on 1,400 of his officers to report to work. At 10 a.m. the crowd started to gather on the Mall and the Eclipse. Shouts of "Stop that Steal" rung out. On the stage near the White House, Donald Trump, Jr., delivered a fiery speech revving up the crowd. Trump's personal attorney Rudy Giuliani called for a "trial by combat," presumably on the understanding that elections in a modern democracy should be decided by medieval jousting rather than voting. Less publicly, he also called senators to encourage them to slow down the electoral vote count.

At 11:57 a.m., Trump took the stage. He repeated the claim that it was a rigged election. Backstage, Trump's inner circle, including his sons and daughter, applauded all the wild assertions and downright lies told on stage. Warning that if Pence allowed the congressional vote to take place later that afternoon Biden would become president, Trump told his supporters. "We're going to walk down Pennsylvania Avenue." His exhortation was slightly delayed by the next phrase, "I love Pennsylvania Avenue," before getting back on message, reminding them of the main point of the action, little more than a mile and half away. "And we're going to the Capitol . . ." He spoke until around 1.10 p.m. He told his supporters to stop the steal, act with strength, and fight like hell.[3]

Even before Trump started speaking, protestors were gathering at the Capitol. At 11:15 a.m. a group of two hundred to three hundred protestors arrived at the Reflecting Pool on the west side of the Capitol. They were joined by thousands more during and after Trump's speech. They began marching toward the Capitol just as the lawmakers were starting to meet in a joint session of Congress to confirm Biden as president. People carried Trump flags, Confederate flags, and some u.s. flags. Some, no doubt after simply keying Georgia into their Internet search, held aloft the flag of Georgia the country, in the mistaken belief that they were holding the flag of Georgia the u.s. state. A man waving a giant Trump sign told those around him that the politicians must pay the ultimate price: "An example needs to be made," he warned. In the crowd were people with megaphones urging the protestors on. Closer to the Capitol, rioters shouted "Let's get them." "It is our America," said one of the relatively few female protestors. It was a motley crew. Some were in camo fatigues, many wore QAnon garb, and one man wore a black T-shirt with the words "Camp Auschwitz" above the image of a skull and crossbones. If the crowd was representative of anything more than itself, it was a cross-section of a scary, hate-filled, conspiracy-addled America.

Trump was still speaking when crowds started to arrive at the west side of the Capitol. The first barricades—little more than three light metal frames that surrounded the base of the Capitol—were toppled around 12.50 a.m. by a crowd egged on by the Proud Boys, part of a small number of militia groups that were active in the organized attack on the Capitol, along with the Oath Keepers and Three Percenters. They reflected the growing prominence of extremist groups encouraged by Trump and formed the hard spine of the insurrection. There was some contact and coordination between the multiple militia groups at the Capitol. The leaders of the Proud Boys and Oath Keepers, for example, were part of a chat group organized by Trump loyalist Roger Stone that also included arch-conspiracist Alex Jones.

There are video images of the assault that show the steps of the east front of the Capitol in the early afternoon.[4] The wide-angle view shows a densely packed crowd massed on the steps. If you look closely, at the center is a tight, single-line formation of people moving in coordinated lockstep. They are dressed similarly in tactical gear with military-style helmets, camouflaged combat jackets, thick gloves, and hardened goggles, and march in single file in a tight formation up the steps to the doors leading to the rotunda on the east side where they force entry into the Capitol. They were members of the right-wing militia group the Oath Keepers.[5]

The Oath Keepers, a far-right anti-government militia group whose members believe they are fighting against a dark conspiracy, was founded in 2009. In 2020 the group had discussed the need to keep Trump in power, as they saw around them a society on the brink of apocalyptic totalitarianism. Their membership at the time of the insurrection was around 5,000. They targeted for membership those with military law enforcement experience; almost two-thirds of current members at the time were from that background or former military. The leader, Stewart Rhodes, used an encrypted messaging system on November 5 to tell his fellow members that a civil war was necessary. He sent a similar message on December 25, December 31, and again on the day before the rally on the Mall. He is reported to have said,

we're going to defend the president, the duly elected president, and we call on him to do what needs to be done to save our country. Because if you don't guys, you're going to be in a bloody, bloody civil war and a bloody—you can call it an insurrection or you can call it a war or fight.[6]

A small group of hardcore members prepared for the event with formal training and weapons handling. They communicated with each other via encrypted messages, phone calls, emails, and on chat rooms. In the lead-up to the insurrection they purchased more than $15,000 worth of firearms and related supplies, including platform rifle sights. They stashed weapons on the other side of the Potomac river, at the Comfort Inn in Arlington, Virginia, where, on January 5, they assembled gun boxes, rifle cases, and suitcases filled with ammunition. Part of the plan was the hope that they would be called upon to enforce Trump's invocation of the Insurrection Act. Other Oath Keepers stayed at different hotels in the area before meeting up on the Mall to make their way up the Capitol steps. After the insurrection, Rhodes was arrested on the charge of sedition. He was at the Capitol that day but said he did not enter the building. Along with ten other Oath Keepers, he was alleged to have planned to stop the lawful transfer of presidential power. In November 2022, he was found guilty of seditious conspiracy and in May 2023 sentenced to eighteen years in prison. One of his deputies, Kelly Meggs, who was in the single-file march up the steps of the Capitol, was sentenced to thirteen years in prison.

The Proud Boys, a neo-fascist, misogynistic, all-male group that promotes political violence, was founded in 2016. Its focus is on recruiting disaffected young White men. Its total membership has never exceeded 5,000, but despite its size, the group has received a lot of attention in recent years. The Republican operative and Trump advisor Roger Stone used its members as security at various events. They were a violent presence at anti-BLM rallies and played a role in fomenting violence in the summer of 2020. At a presidential debate on September 29, 2020, President Trump told them to "stand back and stand by."[7] They came to DC with the expressed intent of stopping the certification of Biden as president and were actively involved in the attack on the Capitol. Video footage shows them playing a key role at strategic barriers and checkpoints. They were on the frontline at these locations confronting the police and egging on the crowds, which they helped to mobilize. At least thirteen Proud Boys were indicted on conspiracy charges. One pled guilty, and the defense lawyers of the others argued that they were not to blame. The fault lay with Trump for inciting the mob and with law enforcement leaders for the failure to adequately prepare for violence. These arguments did not sway the jury. In May 2023, five members were convicted of multiple felonies, and four were found guilty of seditious conspiracy to derail the transfer of power from Trump to Biden.

The Three Percenters are an anti-government movement that was founded in 2008 after the election of the first Black president, Barack Obama. Its membership includes former military and law enforcement. The movement's name comes from the erroneous belief that only 3 percent of colonists fought against the British during the American Revolution. Followers were seen at a rally on January 5 outside the Supreme Court with Roger Stone. On the 6th, Three Percenters were involved in the breach of police barriers, entering the Capitol, and then ransacking and vandalizing offices of members of Congress. In June 2021, six people affiliated with the movement were indicted for conspiracy to obstruct congressional proceedings. One of them, Guy Reffitt, carried a gun and plastic handcuffs with the intent to capture House speaker Nancy Pelosi and Senate majority leader Mitch McConnell and drag them from the building. All six were found guilty, and Reffitt was sentenced to seven years in jail. At his trial, Reffitt tried to excuse his actions by saying "in 2020 I was a little crazy . . . I wasn't thinking clearly."[8] By May 2023 more than 1,000 people had been arrested for the assault on the Capitol.

The United States is a large country with a diverse population. Among its almost 340 million people, there are always the angry and the evil, the unhinged and conspiratorial. The militias and movements mentioned here are part of a long American tradition of political extremism. However, until recent years the extreme tended to remain at the margins of the political landscape. But a distinctive feature of the Trump presidency was the increasing permeability between the fringes and the center of the Republican political establishment, resulting in the mainstreaming of the more extreme, more radical elements of conservative thought and belief. Trump not only stoked fears of a pernicious and evil "deep state" but presented to his followers and voters at large a scenario of "a dramatic final conflict between light and darkness."[9] He tweeted QAnon messages more than 250 times, sometimes twice a day. The intensity of his publicizing of QAnon had an effect. By 2021 almost a third of Republicans believed that Trump was fighting against the child sex traffickers of the Democratic Party and the deep state. Trump repeated messages first espoused on Alex Jones's Infowars and gave direct sustenance to extremist groups such as the Oath Keepers and Proud Boys. His presidency was one long dog whistle, with the occasional more blatant shout-outs, to extreme elements in the country. The Trump presidency normalized extremism and encouraged extremist groups' actions—Trump's support of their beliefs, whether tacit or explicit, played a vital role in inciting them to breach the Capitol.

The City

Washington, DC, is a compromise location. The compromise was forged in the late eighteenth century between three giant figures in the early history of the American Republic: Alexander Hamilton, Thomas Jefferson, and James Madison. The slave-owning Southern planters, led by Jefferson and Madison, wanted a new capital located in the South, away from the banking interests of the North. Hamilton, a vehement critic of slavery, did not want the new capital too far from the business center of New York or in a slave state where it would come under the influence of the plantation oligarchy. However, Hamilton wanted the federal government to pay the states' debts incurred in the Revolutionary War. The two slave owners resisted this idea, fearing that a strong federal state would undermine states' rights and in turn the privileged position of their class. The Compromise of 1790, reached by the three men in a private meeting, agreed that the new federal capital would be in the slave-based plantation economy of the South while the federal government would take over the states' debts. The result was a stronger federal government, and the establishment of a solid basis for the U.S. government to obtain credit from lenders at home and abroad. The U.S. government was seen, from then until now, as a good credit risk and thus able to borrow money at favorable rates. This compromise also established a new capital far from the urban North—with its big towns, mercantile culture, and lively cosmopolitan port cities—and closer to the rural agrarian South and its big landowners and plantation economies built on slave labor.

At the time, there was no obvious site for the capital, so one had to be built. In the interim decade, Philadelphia was the temporary capital, from 1790 to 1800. In a nod to the enormous prestige and influence of revolutionary hero and first president George Washington, the eventual site was located close to his plantation at Mount Vernon, Virginia. A diamond-shaped area of 100 square miles was created from territory in Maryland and Virginia between the Anacostia and Potomac rivers. The new capital was less than 15 miles from Washington's riverside plantation with its extensive slave quarters.

The new city, built on slave labor, was constructed on the traditional territory of local tribes, including the Piscataway, Pamunkey, the Nentego (Nanichoke), Mattaponi, Chickahominy, and Monacan. The land, forcibly taken from them, was their home, their means of living, and the fundamental basis of their cosmology. They were killed off by diseases brought by the White invaders, and some were sold into slavery. The new city, the new nation's capital, was built on a site of ethnic cleansing. Today, little more than 4,000 Indigenous people live in the city. To add insult to calamitous injury, the city's NFL team was, for most of its history going back to 1933, known as the Washington Redskins. The name was only changed in 2020 after public opinion and commercial considerations shifted the stance of Daniel Snyder, arguably one of the most reviled team owners in the NFL, who sold the franchise in May 2023.

The new capital of the young Republic, the District of Columbia (DC), was situated closer to the South than the North. The location guided the city's subsequent development, from its hot muggy climate to its racial attitudes. Before air conditioning was invented and made prevalent, DC was an unpleasant place to live. Thomas Jefferson described the site as "that Indian swamp in the wilderness."

It was also a city compromised at its inception. In Article 1 of the new Constitution the new capital territory was created as a special district, not as a state, because many, including Madison, were worried that if the new capital became a state, it would become too powerful. So, at its founding, DC came under the rule of the U.S. Congress and its inhabitants were deprived of the right to vote for their own political representatives. In an ironic, hypocritical twist, the American Revolutionary slogan of "no taxation without representation" was inverted for the nation's capital where there was taxation without representation.

From the outset then, DC was treated as a special case not worthy of full political representation. The capital of the United States was imagined as an empty space, the setting for national political theater but not a democratic city in its own right. That image of DC as different, not quite the USA, has remained, especially in Congress, where many politicians regularly regale their constituents back home with lurid tales of the idiocy and mendacity of the place. Many position themselves as working in an almost foreign land far from traditional hometown values— until, that is, many of them retire, and they suddenly find the return to the good folks back home sidetracked by the financial lure of becoming a lobbyist in the city. DC is a large feeding trough for well-connected politicians able to monetize their connections and commodify their legislative knowledge. The politician-turned-lobbyist is as much a DC tradition as its Cherry Blossom Festival.

From DC's very beginnings as the capital of the world's leading democracy, its citizens could not vote in congressional and presidential elections. It was only in 1961 that its voters were allowed a say in the Electoral College. It was as if the Southern oligarchy had recreated a political plantation ruled over by a White political elite. Jefferson and Madison would have been proud of the compromise. To this day the federal government still has final jurisdiction over the District. The tensions in this asymmetric relationship would only grow over time as the city became larger, Blacker, and more liberal. Republican politicians still vehemently resist calls for home rule because they fear a reliably Democratic voting bloc.

The constitutional history of Washington, DC, is important in understanding the events of January 6. DC is not a state, and has neither sole nor final jurisdiction over its military guard. Unlike ordinary states where the governor can call out the National Guard as a rapid deployment force to deal with disasters and emergencies, DC falls under the authority of the Pentagon. But, after the fractious summer of 2020, military leaders were wary of the direct use of military force. They were worried that the optics were bad and so hesitated to authorize the use of enough force quickly enough to meet the emerging and mounting threat on the day of the insurrection.

Two other background factors were important. The first is the extremely biased perception by the u.s. military–security complex as to what constitutes a threat to the Republic. Especially since the terrorist attacks on the Pentagon and World Trade Center in 2001, the main threat has been perceived to be Islamic terrorism. That is, the most pressing danger lay abroad as either the foreign Other or the Islamic home-grown radical. The threat from groups outside the majority, such as Arabs, Blacks, or Muslims, was so much easier to characterize as a threat than the White realtor, veteran, or ex-police officer. Seeing Islamic radicalism as the main threat to the Republic deflected attention and resources away from domestic extremist groups, especially those whose members are White, and, especially, middle-aged. The mindset of the military–security establishment was that White Americans were not a threat. So on the day of the march, the Trump supporters were not seen as a major security risk to the capital, the Republic, or, in fact, u.s. democracy. Trump's supporters were given latitude unavailable to minorities.

The second and related factor was the poor, flimsy defenses afforded to the Capitol on the day of the march. The metal barriers surrounding the building were easily pushed aside by the angry, insurgent crowd. In a few key places, the small numbers of Capitol police provided very little or no resistance to the hordes of protestors. Some simply stood around as the crowd thickened and did little to halt the entry of the demonstrators past the outer perimeter.

It was a different story at some of the building entrances on the eastern side of the Capitol and especially on the precipitous west front where the protestors met brave resistance from the police at the crowded access points. Some of the more violent images of the day came from the confrontations at important entrances to the Capitol where police were vastly outnumbered. The police resisted the incursion especially on the steep west side, where they fired tear gas into the crowds. The west front looked like a medieval battle scene as protestors climbed up the walls and the scaffolding of the temporary erections for the inauguration, a marauding horde against a lightly guarded fortress. The steep side of the building was filled with clambering insurrectionists trying to break in at the tunnels and doors. They used bear spray, tasers, shields and sticks, chairs, and batons against the police guarding the entrances and tunnels.

The complex was first breached at around 2 p.m. Eventually the building was breached in eight locations, and the police officers at those sites were dragged, beaten, sprayed, electrocuted with tasers, and eventually overwhelmed. On the east side of the Capitol, Oath Keepers marched single file up the steps to the doors leading to the rotunda. At around 2.30 p.m. they forced entry into the Capitol. Other insurrectionists climbed the steps and broke through the doors leading directly into the building.

The size of the violent mob that made its way into the Capitol is estimated at between 2,000 and 2,500. A total of 150 police were injured. One officer, Brian Sicknick, died after being sprayed with mace or bear spray and four officers later died by suicide. A protestor, Ashli Babbitt, was shot by a police officer as she tried to enter the Capitol. One protestor had a heart attack and another was crushed to death by the crowd.[10]

As the fight raged between insurgents and police outside, the constitutional process was playing out inside. Pence entered the house chamber to preside over the counting of electoral votes just after the outer perimeter barriers were breached. At 1.30 p.m. Mitch McConnell, Republican leader of the Senate, said that if the senators ruled to overturn the Electoral College votes "it would damage our Republic forever." It seemed he was having a late change of heart. In the months leading up that day he did little to squash the Big Lie.

With the security situation rapidly deteriorating, Mayor Bowser requested additional guard forces from Secretary of the Army Ryan McCarthy. The National Guard had not yet been authorized. By 1:50 p.m., the commander of the DC police force declared a riot. Just after 2 p.m. Secret Service agents rushed Pence from the Senate chamber to safety. Soon afterwards, Nancy Pelosi, a particular target of many of the more violent insurgents, was also removed from the chamber. At 2:29 p.m., the session was finally recessed as politicians and their staff fled for safety.

Capitol police and staffers barricaded the main entrance leading into the House as lawmakers continued to evacuate. At 2:44 p.m. a Capitol police officer guarding a door on the east side shot and fatally wounded a rioter. At 2:52 p.m. the first FBI SWAT team entered the building. Only at 4.10 p.m. did the acting defense secretary, Christopher Miller, authorize field activation of the 1,100-member DC National Guard. By 5:40 p.m., 150 members of the DC guard arrived at the Capitol. A citywide curfew was declared starting at 6:00 p.m., which gave the authorities the power to arrest people still out and about after that time. By 6:14 p.m. police and the National Guard had established a perimeter around the building. The Capitol was declared secure at 8 p.m. Six minutes later, the Senate was called back into session, followed by the House. The session lasted into the night and into the early hours of the next morning. At 4.42 a.m., on January 7, Joe Biden was declared president elect.

Trump watched the unfolding events on a television screen in the White House for hours. As the violence increased, his daughter, one of his sons, and minority House leader Kevin McCarthy asked him to stop the violence. He did nothing. While most looked on the mayhem and violence and saw social breakdown, what Trump saw was affirmation. He could see only people who wanted him to remain president. Rather than a plea to the protestors to call off the assault, all he could muster was a request that the "good people" go home.

There are many reasons for the failure to defend the Capitol on January 6. The Capitol was lightly policed and defenses were minimally hardened around the complex. There was not enough police protection for the peaceful transfer of power even though the march had been planned for weeks and the presence of violent extremist groups in Trump's support base was well known. I will suggest three reasons for this dramatic security failure.

First, White privilege. The demonstrators were mainly White, so in the minds of many, they were considered "real" Americans. Their race and political persuasion were not perceived as a threat to the established order. This was not a BLM march filled with angry young Black people. Because this crowd represented "White America," it was not taken seriously as a threat to the established order; it was the established order.

Second, there was the unique constitutional position of Washington, DC. The people who oversee the Capitol's police, the House and Senate sergeants at arms, also answer to the House speaker and Senate majority leader. Traditionally these leadership politicians have wanted only light security in the Capitol to maintain the idea of an accessible democracy. Politicians want to be able to give interviews to the press in order to get their message across—and in the case of Republican Senator Josh Hawley, give a clenched fist salute to assembled MAGA supporters on the morning of January 6. So outside of immediate terrorist threats—and MAGA supporters were not considered a threat for reasons we just noted—the Capitol was less guarded than it probably should have been in these hyperpartisan times, as politicians today try to balance security with democratic accessibility and contact with the press.

Third, there was a confusing and confused command structure. The Capitol has its own police force whose only real role is to protect the building and its occupants. It failed, in part, because the Capitol Police is an organization that lacks transparency, public scrutiny, or stringent oversight. It has a perplexing chain of command involving a three-member board, four oversight committees, and 535 members of Congress who all want public access to their offices. The upper management was negligent in assessing the threat and failed to have a coherent and proportional plan in place to ensure the security of the Capitol in a circumstance precisely like this one—all despite the prior warning from multiple intelligence reports that suggested such a threat was possible. The FBI, the Department of Homeland Security, and even the Capitol Police's own intelligence unit had been monitoring right-wing extremists for weeks as they armed and prepared to attack the capital. Somehow this information did not make its way up the chain of command. The chief of the Capitol Police later claimed that he was given no warning of this disturbing intelligence. The Pentagon leadership had a sense that this was not a dangerous crowd, it was White people after all— not young radicals, antifa, or Black people demanding rights and accountability for police brutality and murders. This crowd was made up of ex-police officers, veterans, serving politicians, Christian dads. They were, for many in authority, the real America. You only heavily police those who threaten the existing order, not those who are the existing order.

Despite the intelligence reports, the possibility of violence was not met with a coherent, coordinated response. And the city's inability to call out its own National Guard (in contrast to all other states) meant that it was at a disadvantage. The military was heavily criticized for its actions in DC over the preceding summer when innocent protestors had been tear-gassed in Lafayette Square so that Trump, with top military leadership by his side, could have his shallow photo opportunity. To avoid another public relations disaster, especially against a White Republican crowd, the Pentagon hesitated and prevaricated.

At around 1.30 p.m. Mayor Bowser asked for National Guard assistance in a call with the then secretary of the army, Ryan McCarthy. He presumably ran it up the chain of command. The request was not acted upon for at least three hours afterwards. The Capitol Police chief at the time, Steven Sund, recalls that he sent an urgent request for help to the Pentagon around 2:30 p.m.[11] But it took the Pentagon officials another two hours at a crucial juncture to allow the National Guard to come to the capital. The army secretary only notified the leader of the Washington National Guard by phone at 4:35 p.m. that he was now authorized to send in troops. The leader of the guard, Major General William Walker, told senators later at a hearing that it was only at 5:08 p.m. that he received approval to deploy the troops. The first of them arrived at 5:40 p.m. Most of the DC National Guard did not arrive at the scene until just after 6:00 p.m. Police from New Jersey, over a hundred miles and three states away, got there sooner than the DC National Guardsmen located less than a few miles from the Capitol. In the aftermath, the Pentagon, ever nimble in avoiding responsibility, tried to shift the blame for the delayed response onto the Washington National Guard. The Pentagon took more than three hours to send National Guard troops to aid DC and Capitol police at a time of an insurrectionist attack on the Capitol.

The Assault: Insurrection as Performance

The video images of the assault are compelling. They show a small, disciplined paramilitary group at the very center of an amorphous crowd. The image distills the basic nature of the insurrection. There was a small nexus of organizers that included the president, Republican politicians, and political operatives. On the ground that day were paramilitary equivalents: the right-wing militia groups, the Oath Keepers, Three Percenters, and Proud Boys. This small core of Trump support had shared a desire and a plan to undermine the election and install a *caudillo* in place of the duly elected president.

Then there was a larger periphery, the general crowd, called to DC by their president and their gut feeling, fueled by lies and deception that the election had been stolen. They were an inchoate mass with no coherent plan. They included the sad, the mad, and the bad. They were mainly White, middle-income earners, and middle-aged. They were retired, unemployed, blue-, and white-collar workers. They felt they were the marginalized and ignored, a cultural underclass whose leader was no longer president.

Many members of the crowd who assembled that day in DC and who walked up the Mall to the Capitol saw themselves as patriots, echoing the revolutionary nature of America's inception and its overthrow of tyranny. It was a repeat of sorts, but it is important to recall the observation of Karl Marx, who noted that history does repeat itself, but the second time as farce. Most of those who entered the Capitol had no ties to extremist groups. Very few had a plan to execute politicians. Most came to DC to show support for Trump and some may have intended to do little more than walk to the Capitol. Many had no real plan of any kind other than to turn up in support of Trump's "victory," a signaling of a distorted sense of patriotism. Most of the 20,000 or so who attended the march and the approximately 2,500 who entered the Capitol were a thick mass of incoherent anger encasing a core terrorist spine.

It could be described as a race riot. The mob was overwhelmingly White, middle-aged, and male. Their profile made them less of a threat in the eyes of many in authority that day. They were self-described patriots. But by marching on the capital and trying to overturn the result of a democratic election they were not defending anything other than their willful expression of White power. One disturbing image was of a man with a large Confederate flag on his shoulder, the battle flag of a rebellion against the Republic, paraded through the seat of elected power. A reminder, if the summer of 2020 had not already pressed the claim, that racism was alive and well. The Confederate flag along with Trump flags were clearly visible, intermingling in an expression of the White anger and White resentment that had fueled support for Trump since his run for the presidency.

When they broke through the flimsy defenses, many of the insurrectionists, unsure of exactly what to do next, simply milled around. Some took selfies. Others posted their exploits on social media. Most were caught up in the heat of the moment, carried by the swell of the crowd and deposited in the building where they seemed slightly stunned to find they were in the Capitol. In one video you can hear someone ask as they enter the Senate chamber, "What's the plan?" Someone is heard saying "I have no idea." He spoke for many.

Some rifled through the desks of senators, taking photos of documents. Others went through the halls trying to open the closed doors shielding frightened politicians and their terrified staff. Some were looking for senior politicians, especially Nancy Pelosi, Mitch McConnell, and Mike Pence. Most simply wandered around. Some committed acts of vandalism, breaking furniture, smashing signs, scattering papers, rifling through drawers, sitting in the chairs of elected representatives, defecating in the corridors: the more obvious acts of transgression. They sat on ceremonial chairs and put their feet up on desks. It was both deeply menacing and vaguely comical. Most of the participants weren't exactly sure what to do or how to act. It was a planned attack by a small, focused, and determined minority as much as a mindless mob, some of whom had stumbled almost by accident into the halls of power. Some tweeted and livestreamed, others wore badges that were used to identify them later in legal proceedings. There were two elements, the organized and the disorganized, making it both insurrectionary and farcical. The violent intent of conspiracists was combined with the random anarchy of the mob. Both shared the political incoherence of the extreme right and its lauding of violence as the main form of civic participation. It was not revolutionary in the sense of establishing a new order. The violence was not a means to an end, it was the more fascistic expression of violence as a form of personal expression.[12]

For many there seemed no goal other than presence at the protest itself. A simmering resentment, years in the making, was brought to the boil. It was not so much a political demonstration as a primal scream of the misogynistic, the racist, the confused, the unhinged, and the unmoored. The participants included a hard core of violent extremists, with distinct strategies and agreed-upon tactics, as well as a larger crowd of the angry and the ostensibly patriotic: a motley crew brought to the event by an eagerness to do something and be part of something bigger than themselves.

Klete Keller's 6-foot 6-inch towering frame was captured in a photograph of the melee in the rotunda. He was easily recognizable to those who knew him, not only because of his striking height but the fact that he wore a Team USA jacket with the U.S. Olympic Patch on his left shoulder. Keller was a genuine Olympic star who over the course of three Olympics in Sydney, Athens, and Beijing won five medals. He is perhaps not the likeliest of Trump supporters, yet in January 2021 he was charged in the u.s. District Court with trespass, violent entry, disorderly conduct, and obstructing law enforcement. He pled guilty. Like many in the crowd, he felt adrift. Although he could claim some truly impressive athletic achievements, his post-Olympic story is one of dislocation. After his retirement from competitive swimming in 2008, he struggled. He was divorced, jobless, and for a while homeless. He slept in a car in the parking lots of Wal-Marts and rest stops. People who knew him described him as a lost soul long before Trump rose to power, perhaps unable to adjust to a normal life after the robust and tightly choreographed schedule of an Olympic athlete. But with the rise of Trump, this lost soul found a new community led by a charismatic leader. Like many others in the United States, he fell under the spell of Trump.[13]

At least nineteen state and local officials took part in the insurrection, including the Otero County Commissioner of New Mexico, a state legislator from West Virginia, a state representative from Missouri, a state senator from Virginia, and a county commissioner from New Jersey. The insurrectionists also included retired and active military and current and former police officers. Almost 20 percent of those arrested at the Capitol were former or active-duty military. Most police unions backed Trump in 2020.

As well as an overrepresentation of the military and police, there was a sprinkling of the extreme right. One of the insurrectionist's was a ucla student, Christian Secor, who belonged to a far-right, White supremacist group known as America First. He entered the west side of the building at 2.26 p.m., walked through the offices, and then overwhelmed three police officers trying to bar doors on the building's east side. He entered the Senate floor at 2:49 p.m. and sat in the seat that just half an hour previously had been occupied by Vice President Pence.[14] Later, he was expelled from UCLA and in October 2022 he was sentenced to three and a half years in prison after he pleaded guilty to the obstruction of an official proceeding.

The day had an anarchic and performative character. Some, like the man who put his feet up on Nancy Pelosi's office chair, combined both elements. His name was Richard Barnett. His nickname was Bigo. Later in court, he said he was pushed into the building by the mob and then wandered around it only to find himself in the House speaker's office, where he sat back in the chair, put his heavy work boots on the desk, and wrote, "Nancy, Bigo was here you bitch." Barnett is an interesting case, because in many ways his story was shared by many others. In his small hometown in Arkansas, he got most of his news from the Internet. The websites he frequented throughout 2020 told him of a country beset with race riots, burning buildings, and the killing of innocent people. He believed the Big Lie and decided to come to Washington. He came prepared. He stopped off at Bass Pro shops and bought six walkie talkies, canisters of pepper spray, and a 950,000-volt stun gun. It's fair to say that his claims of innocence seem odd considering the objects in his possession. And like many insurrectionists fed a steady diet of conspiracy theories, he told reporters at his trial that he still believed the election was a fraud, that Trump had won and that the political left is out to destroy the Constitution. In May 2023 he was sentenced to four and a half years in prison.

And who can forget the Trickster, Jake Angeli, also known as Jacob Chansley, one of the first people to enter the Capitol?

Most people will remember him more by his costume than his name. He wore a cape made of coyote fur and buffalo horns, and carried a 6-foot spear with an American flag attached. He was shirtless, so people could see his elaborate tattoos of Nordic design reminiscent of Viking warriors (adopted in recent years by right-wing fascist groups). His face was painted. He had a demonic, yet strangely unthreatening demeanor that combined the campiness of a make-believe Hun invader and wannabe Viking warrior with the look of a lost extra on a film set. It came as no surprise that he still lived with his mother. In November 2023 he pleaded guilty to obstruction and was sentenced to 41 months in prison. His mother told authorities that he required organic food while incarcerated.

Trump had urged his supporters to march on the Capitol, promising that things were "going to be wild." Angeli/Chansley was the very embodiment of the "performative wild." He reminded me of those frontier figures who, early in America's history, were halfway between civilization and the wilderness, eschewing the banality of the domesticated and prone to violence. Chansley played up to the role of archetypal figure of American mythology, and embodied the theatrical and gestural, combining wildness, shamanism, and paganism, all wrapped around a vague political agenda. Less a political activist, he was more like a cameo from a badly directed Wagnerian opera. As he walked the halls of Congress, he was a reminder of the barbarian quality of Trump's support but also the wildman that lies at the very heart of American civilization.

The Capitol mob, unsurprisingly, included misogynists. One man who did not hide his involvement in the insurrec-tion was West Virginia delegate Derrick Evans, who swore his oath of office on December 14, 2020, at the state capital of Charleston. He had a long history of harassing women and staff at local abortion clinics. One clinic had to build a 10-foot fence to deter him. Clinic volunteers had to obtain a restraining order against him for stalking them and livestreaming their personal details. He targeted women and especially women of color, and labeled one supporter of LGBTQ+ rights as satanic. Colleagues at Virginia Tech, where he worked as an assistant coach for the football team, said he constantly demeaned women. While participating in the insurrection, he live-streamed his involvement, screaming "Derrick Evans is in the Capitol." He was later convicted of civil disorder and sentenced to three months in prison. On January 6, 2023, exactly two years later, he announced his candidacy as a Republican for the West Virginia first congressional district.

Jenna Ryan flew into Washington on a private jet, but despite this surface appearance of affluence, she, like many others, had money issues. Nearly 60 percent of the people arrested had liens for unpaid federal taxes.[15] Ryan's financial troubles included bankruptcies, evictions, and foreclosures. She had filed for bankruptcy in 2012 and had an outstanding $37,000 lien for unpaid federal taxes when she arrived at the Capitol. She posted photos of herself at the event and, not wanting to pass up the commercial opportunity afforded by the exposure, tagged the images with the message "JennaRyan for your Realtor." She was, predictably, easily identified and brought to trial, where she was sentenced to sixty days in jail. She is now back to selling real estate.

Bolstering the support for Trump were class resentment, racial prejudice, and cultural animosity. But there was also an important economic dimension. Many of the participants lived in the liminal area of economic insecurity, part of the declining middle class (some even of the upper class) faced with the precarity of struggling to maintain financial viability. Many of the protestors had debts and unpaid tax bills. This fits in with research about extremist groups which show it is often people in the middle of society—those who are neither wealthy enough to be considered "successful" in American terms nor trapped in poverty—who feel they are losing status and power that are especially attracted to the rhetoric of authoritarian populism.[16] A powerful predictor of support for the far right in later life is the experience of being a child living through parents' unemployment, bankruptcy, or falling behind in tax payments. The sense of precarity in a society reinforces a sense of loss.[17] Riley June Williams was found guilty of two felonies for her role in the Capitol insurrection. Court records show that her parents had filed for bankruptcy when she was a child. Money worries are not an excuse, obviously, but they were an accelerant to the rage, the anger, and the resentment.

In one interesting study, the economic historian John Komlos looked up the zip code addresses of more than 933 people who were arrested after the Capitol.[18] He found that, at least according to the average income of their neighborhood according to the u.s. Census, the vast majority of those arrested were in the middle-income range, with only a few from neighborhoods with an average personal income of less than $15,000 per person. Those from lower-income neighborhoods, as well as those from neighborhoods with an estimated annual household income above $100,000, were underrepresented among the insurrectionists. The vast majority lived in neighborhoods with average household incomes between $35,000 and $100,000. Almost 41 percent of insurrectionists resided in this category yet in the u.s population they constitute only 21 percent of the total. The study is not perfect, it assumes the neighborhood level closely approximates the household level of income. There is always the danger of ecological fallacy, the mistake that individual characteristics can be read off from group characteristics. Every zip code has a range of income levels. It could be that those with lower incomes would be especially angry if comparing their lot with their more affluent neighbors. We should be careful when interpreting the individual based on the group. Given this proviso, Komlos's findings still suggest that it was not so much lack of income, or level of poverty, that generated the energy to come to the Capitol on January 6. It was a White middle-class rage fueled by a lessening of their economic power, social status, and cultural standing. Not all hard-pressed, middle-income people were insurrectionists, but the fact that many of them came from the middle class, I think, tells us about the growing unease and feeling of being decentered that this class, especially those without a college degree, have experienced in recent decades. Perceived economic uncertainty, political alienation, and cultural marginalization are some of the larger structural conditions behind the insurrection. Trump appealed to this precarious group disconnected from rising affluence, threatened by cultural diversity, and alienated from normal political discourse. The more motivated of them turned up on January 6 to subvert the election results to keep him in power.

8

Aftermath

As Trump supporters made their way to the Capitol on January 6, Republican representative Paul Gosar and Republican senator Ted Cruz were objecting to the counting of the electoral ballots from Arizona. They demanded an emergency audit. Since state tallies were announced alphabetically, Arizona gave an early opportunity to advance the coup. Deliberations inside the Capitol were then overshadowed and then undermined by events outside the building. By 2 p.m. the demonstrators overpowered the Capitol police and entered the building. At 2:29 p.m., as demonstrators breached the building's security, so the Senate and then the House went into recess as members were rushed to safety. One of the Republican senators, Josh Hawley, who saluted and ginned up the crowd on his entrance into the Capitol, was later seen on video scurrying away from the mob as fast as his tight-trousered legs could carry him. By 3 p.m., the insurrectionists had swarmed into the Senate chamber.

Trump watched these events on television yet refused to send additional police or troops to quell the violence. Eventually, reinforcements came from the National Guard. By the early evening, the Capitol had been reclaimed, the debris removed, and Congress returned to business. Institutional norms were reestablished.

Members of the House and Senate, who only hours earlier had donned gas masks, barricaded their offices, and crouched under their desks, were gathered once more as the joint session was called to order. At 8 p.m., the vote continued as the ballots of the electors were read out in alphabetical order by tellers. There was a lot of speechifying, so it was only at a little before 4 a.m. in the early hours of the next day, January 7, that Pence announced the result of the electoral votes, 306 for Biden and 232 for Trump. Having received more than the requisite 270 electoral votes, Biden's electoral victory was formally confirmed. Later, on January 20, with a return to protocol traditions, his inauguration as the 46th President of the USA took place on the west side of the Capitol, the scene of the most violent confrontations of the insurrection.

In one sense, then, after months of an attempted coup and hours of insurrectionist mayhem, the institution of government returned to normal.

Not quite.

The Big Lie continued to contaminate the body politic. During that night of deliberations, the House and Senate met separately. Only one House member and one senator needed to object to trigger hours of debate. Mere hours after the searing violence of the insurrection, 147 Republicans in the House and Senate supported one or both objections to Electoral College counts in Arizona and Pennsylvania; they included the leader of the House Republicans, Kevin McCarthy, later to become speaker, and seven of his leadership team, including Jim Jordan, the ranking Republican member, and after the 2022 midterms, the chair of the House Judiciary Committee.

Six senators voted to sustain the challenge to the Arizona electors: Josh Hawley of Missouri, Ted Cruz of Texas, Tommy

Tuberville of Alabama, Cindy Hyde-Smith of Mississippi, Roger Marshall of Kansas, and John Kennedy from Louisiana. These six politicians plus two more—Cynthia Lummis of Wyoming and Rick Scott of Florida—voted to overturn the results in Pennsylvania. One of Trump's most persistent critics within conservative circles was the late Michael Gerson, a columnist for the *Washington Post*. In numerous opinion pieces he excoriated Republicans like these for offering no resistance to Trump's creeping authoritarianism and argued that the core political commitment in the United States should be to a system of self-government based on the rule of law and the protection of rights. He believed that by not defending procedural democracy, Republican politicians had abandoned any commitment to democratic ideals.[1]

The Big Lie continues to swirl around political discourse in the country. Polls suggest a majority of Republican voters believe Trump won the election, and deniers continue to be voted into office. In a poll taken one year afterwards, close to 80 percent of Republicans continued to believe that the 2020 election was stolen.[2]

With one of the only two political parties in the country supporting such claims, the legitimation crisis continues to haunt the country. The United States is a nation where a significant minority believe the government is illegitimate. Having established this powerful conspiracy narrative, many will continue to believe this as long their party of choice continues to lose elections. The normal operations of politics cease to function once rancor, distrust, and extreme partisanship displace them. By consequence, the improvement of the citizenry's general welfare continues to be ignored and governing degrades into a form of political vendetta.

A Reckoning?

There was also an official reckoning of sorts. The January 6th committee was established by Congress on June 30, 2021, and took evidence over the next eighteen months. The initial idea was to have seven Democrats and six Republicans involved in proceedings, but when Nancy Pelosi refused to sit two Republican nominees who had supported the insurrection, the Republican leader McCarthy withdrew his party's formal participation. Only two Republicans, Liz Cheney and Adam Kinzinger, agreed to serve, and both were ostracized by their Party for their participation.

The report from the committee makes for interesting reading and provides striking insights.[3] It found that Trump obstructed official proceedings, conspired to defraud the nation, made false statements, and incited and assisted insurrection. It shows that Trump was warned well beforehand about the dangers of the crowd on January 6 getting out of control. One of his most loyal advisers, Hope Hicks, advised him several times to urge the demonstrators to keep the event peaceful.

What emerges from the report is that the prime motivation for Trump's actions was to avoid being seen as a loser. He told the White House chief of staff, Mark Meadows, "I don't want people to know we've lost . . . this is embarrassing." If Trump had admitted that the election was lawful, it would have been tantamount to publicly admitting that he had lost. Democracy was shaken, seven people died, and 114 law enforcement officers were injured, all because Trump did not want to be seen as a failure.

The report, in its catalog of events, makes clear that the president sought to undermine the American system of electoral democracy. Trump had long campaigned against the legitimacy of American elections, and continued to do so even after he won. In the final days of Trump's administration, the White House was emptied of talent, leaving only hangers-on like Rudy Giuliani, Sidney Powell, Mike Lindell, and John Eastman to confirm and reinforce Trump's wildest conspiracies. Trump's lawyers filed 62 federal and state lawsuits. They lost all but one and that was on a minor technical matter. The attempted coup tactic, concocted by Eastman, was the declaration that voting in seven states was in dispute. Trump even tried to intimidate governors and local election officials. On January 5, Trump met with Pence at the White House and pressured him to call for a ten-day recess and send the slates back to the disputed states. Pence refused.

The final report did a good job of highlighting the culpability of Donald Trump in the attempted coup and in fomenting the insurrection. It is a narrow indictment, with eight criminal referrals. But it missed an opportunity to examine the wider context. The committee's final report focused overmuch on the role that Donald Trump played. It read, as it was probably meant to be read, as the starting point for a DOJ investigation. The wider role played by Republicans in the coup leading up to January 6 and in then promoting the insurrection itself was largely ignored. The journalist Ron Brownstein noted that the report increased the odds that Trump will face accountability, "but diminished the prospect of a complete reckoning within the GOP."[4] The report said little about the large number of Republican members and elected representatives who took part in the attempt to undermine a democratic election, including the seventeen republican state attorneys who signed on to a bogus lawsuit to undermine the election results in key states, the 147 Republican members of Congress who voted to reject the election results, and the almost three hundred Republicans who promoted the Big Lie and ran for office in November 2022. One baffled conservative, barely able to believe what had happened to his party, entitled his op-ed, "A Man Who Contemplated a Military Coup Against the Constitution is Approved of By More than 80 Percent of Republicans."[5]

The commission's published findings did little to shed light on the role of social media and the pernicious impact of social media companies' unwillingness to stop the violent rhetoric and hate-filled speech spouted by Trump's followers, and the transmission of conspiracy theories in general and the Big Lie in particular. A report from the *Washington Post* suggested that the committee leaders were concerned about not offending powerful tech companies and so said little about holding social media companies accountable for their role in the insurrection. Most members wanted to keep the focus on Trump, and one Democratic member, whose district included Silicon Valley, also vigorously resisted efforts to focus on social media companies.[6]

The report's exclusive focus on the role of Donald Trump ignored a deeper background of growing polarization, mounting distrust of government, increasing inequality, and how conspiracy theories had entered the mainstream. The legalistic findings were set against an unexamined political background. It did not explore what Harvard academic Jill Lepore describes as "the fertile ground of political and social turmoil."[7] It included no discussion of why 20 percent of Americans, and most Republicans, still believe that the election was stolen. The report depicted a country with no past, no future, just an eternal present.

The Longer Term

As the time of writing, only a couple of years since the event, it is difficult to fully understand the longer-term implications of the attempted coup and the insurrection. Both failed to achieve their objective. Biden was declared the winner and became the 46th President. Political norms were reestablished. Sort of. The Republic showed resilience in the face of a direct attack. This time not from jihadists or radical Islamists, but from an elected president and significant numbers of one of the two main political parties.

Yet, those who argue for the resilience of the Republic should be aware that it was a close-run thing. Trump was an authoritarian leader, but a lazy, unfocused one, easily distracted. A more determined leader may have been successful, and the insurrection may well have stopped the confirmation of Biden as president, and possibly in a more vicious manner. If Mike Pence or Nancy Pelosi or any other politician had been caught by the extremists, there was a very real possibility of violence. What would have happened, say, if Pence had been killed or taken hostage? The certification would have been delayed, creating a major rupturing of the political order and perhaps a catastrophic constitutional crisis. In such political upheaval, it is easy to envision that the election would have been returned to the states and Democratic electoral victories overturned by Republican-dominated legislatures in key states such as Arizona and Pennsylvania, triggering a precipitous fall into political chaos and constitutional uncertainty. It is not beyond the bounds of possibility to imagine this scenario. It was what the elected president at the time and significant members of the Republican political elite were working to achieve. So, there should be a sense of relief that politics eventually returned to normal, since it was neither guaranteed nor obvious that it would. A possibly fatal body blow to democracy was probably closer than many people can ever imagine.

The Republican Party Continues to Do Crazy

In the 1976 presidential election, Democrat Jimmy Carter won 50 percent of the evangelical vote. Fast forward to 2020 and Donald Trump won close to 80 percent of the evangelical vote. In 1976 there were few Republican officials in the South, but by 2020 the region was reliably Republican. The party changed, becoming more White, more evangelical, and more entrenched in the South. It became more populist as the traditional values of the business wing of small government and low taxes were replaced by an emphasis on cultural issues and a greater openness to conspiracy theories.

The Republican Party has different elements. Its traditional business wing is concerned with limiting taxes on business, reducing government regulations, and resisting redistributional social and economic policies. But in the 2009 financial crisis, the ultimate cost of dismantling regulatory systems and giving finance capital free rein was brought to the fore. It was a moral hazard on steroids. The risky lending practices of financial institutions undermined not only the housing mortgage market but indeed the national and global economy. The public's distaste at the government for bailing out the banks was palpable and led to the rise of the Tea Party.

The Party's foreign policy establishment pushed for an aggressive posture in the world, and advocated for large amounts of military spending and an abrasive attitude toward the Soviet Union and then later Russia. The Republicans espousing this view reached their pinnacle of influence with the invasion of Iraq. They believed the United States could impose its will on the world order. The fiasco of the Iraq War and the long, expensive, and failed occupation of Afghanistan undercut their position and ultimately the belief in America's imperial might.

The traditional elites who had shaped the domestic and foreign policy agenda in the Republican Party were losing influence. Even leaders of the traditional Republican John McCain's presidential election campaign of 2008 felt the need to add the Alaska populist, Sarah Palin, to provide something new: a fresh, young, female vice-presidential candidate. The rapid elevation of Palin's approval ratings among the Republican base was perhaps an early hint of the emerging populist strain in the Republican Party. The Republican defeat in the 2008 presidential elections occasioned a brief introspection as some began to look at how the Party could expand its base and offer an effective alternative to the Democratic hold on America. The anxiety did not last long, as the Tea Party and an energized base moved the party into the populist and conspiratorial. This shift was marked by the defeat of House Leader Eric Cantor in a Republican primary in 2014 by a right-wing populist challenger. The implications were immediately recognized by Republican hopefuls and seasoned old-timers; to gain or maintain support it was essential to tack to the populist right. This shift was fueled by the right-wing media ecosystem that had developed in the 1990s to give a platform to the entrepreneurs of rage and resentment, the purveyors of American decline, who took it upon themselves to unveil the insidious inner forces undermining the great Republic.

These ideas gained traction from a hard-pressed American middle class who felt that they were being denied their place in American society.

To justify their new, more extremist position Republicans had to create a bogeyman, someone or something to fear. They constantly repeated the terms "socialist takeover," "extreme left wing," and most bizarrely of all "communist takeover." The claims of rampant socialism and creeping communism were expressed sincerely in a country with one of the weakest social welfare systems, and one of the lowest tax rates for the wealthy. American exceptionalism sees tax proposals as left-wing agendas and healthcare for all as a communist plot. While the rest of the world moves toward some form of general agreement between the role of government and private markets, with an acknowledgement of the responsibility of the very wealthy to pay their fair share, the United States carries on as if the debate is still about resisting George III or Joseph Stalin.

The symbiosis between the Republican and partisan news organizations was clearly revealed when one of the first acts of the new Republican House speaker in the Congress of 2023 was to release hours of CCTV coverage of the insurrection to the media, and initially only to Tucker Carlson of Fox News, who carefully cherry-picked the material to show a benign picture of the insurrectionists as peaceful visitors, innocent tourists. The Big Lie was turning into the False Narrative.

The populist strain was combined with the conspiratorial too in the election of Marjorie Taylor Green in the 2020 congressional elections. On the first day of the new congressional session on January 3, 2021, she walked into the Capitol building wearing a black mask covering her mouth with white lettering that spelled out *Trump Won*. She had won handily in a House district in Georgia even though, or indeed even because, she believed in QAnon conspiracies and had a long history of not only tweeting incendiary remarks, but cruelly harassing others, such as on one occasion a survivor of the Parkland school shooting of 2018. She was often seen at gun rallies. She had tweeted comments declaring the Democratic Party to be a satanic child-trafficking ring whose members drink the blood of children. She claimed that shootings in Las Vegas in 2017, at Parkland school in 2018, and at a mosque in New Zealand in 2019 were all false flag events purposely staged by those who wanted to promote gun control. She also questioned the 9/11 terrorist attacks. On Wednesday, March 7, 2023, the Republican House leader appointed her as speaker pro tempore. On that day she called the chamber to order and then the clerk read out the proclamation of her role as the honorary temporary speaker. On that day a confirmed conspiracist was the leader of the House.

Conspiracy Is Alive and Well

Conspiracies have leapt from the edge to the mainstream of political discourse. This mainstreaming is a result of easy diffusion through the Internet and the growing suspicion of authority.[8] For the Republicans, it started with the Barack Obama birther campaign and ended up with a majority of Republican voters believing the election was stolen. And it continued after the insurrection. When, in March 2022, Republican senators quizzed Ketanji Brown Jackson at her Supreme Court nomination hearing, they frequently alluded to her as soft on child pornography. Her sentencing history was no different from previous Republican nominees for federal judgeships. Their questioning can only be understood in the full context of the conspiracy theories of QAnon and Infowars, which imagine that Democrats run organized child abuse cabals. The Republican senators were signaling to their base that they were on their guard against such horrors.

The spread of conspiracies from the periphery to the mainstream and their easy transmission across a range of media platforms make this a dangerous time. There is a significant portion of the population feeling marginalized, alienated, and ignored by a political and economic system that seems unable to meet many of their basic needs. If one of the major political parties also believes it is fighting child molesters and communist conspiracies, then normal politics is suspended. Bipartisanship is tantamount to treason. The conspiratorial fringe is like a deadly virus that has entered the nation's bloodstream. In these conspiratorial communities, hermetically sealed from recognizable truth and empirical reality, but also given oxygen by a mainstream party, anger and resentment are rife and agitation to action is easy to incite. Wild and dangerous theories are repeated and exaggerated rather than examined or contested.

Constitutional Crisis

What the coup and insurrection revealed was the constitutional messiness of the United States. Long lauded as a work of political genius, the u.s. Constitution is in fact a ramshackle device reaching the end of, if it hasn't already outlived, its suitability for the modern age. Lifetime-appointed Supreme Court justices chosen after a judicial death or retirement by whoever is president at that random time, an Electoral College long past its sell-by date, a gerrymandered electoral system where voter suppression is rampant, and a lack of institutional guidelines for the transition from one administration to another: all are part of a sclerotic political system that needs not only updating for the modern era but upgrading for a more partisan, dangerous world.

The United States is not a democracy. It is a republic where the will of the people is mediated though multiple levels and different spheres of government. The United States, despite oft-repeated claims to the contrary, especially by its detractors eager to pass it off as an ingenue, has one of the oldest functioning political systems in the world. Portugal as a country has existed for almost eight hundred years but its form of government and its system of governance has changed radically. In that regard, Portugal of today is very different from Portugal of over two hundred years ago, similarly with the United Kingdom and France. The United States' political system, in contrast, is more than two hundred years old. While the Founding Fathers may not recognize the popular culture of our contemporary USA, they would immediately recognize the basic structure of the system of government. There is even an originalist doctrine that contends that we should base our laws on the original intentions of the Founding Fathers and keep a straight line between then and now. Originalism is an ideological hoax, a slippery plastic concept shaped to justify contemporary political positions, but what is interesting is its source of ideological justification. It lays claim to the original point of constitutional conception rather than, like many other legal doctrines, looking to the present or the future. It is the legalistic equivalent of denying evolution and adopting Creationism.

There remains remarkable persistence between the original constitutional arrangements and the present. And that is part of the problem. A first-past-the-post voting system, arcane voting procedures, the political weight given to small, unrepresentative states: there exists a mounting democratic deficit of an ageing governance framework. Such characteristics may not in themselves be major problems for a functioning democracy but collectively they constitute a political system that is not equal to the demands of current needs and conditions.

The United States and the World

Trump, the coup, and the insurrection had international dimensions. It was part of a rightward shift and rise of authoritarian populism that has also been evident recently in Hungary, Poland, and Turkey. Trump was part of this movement, a leader who used terms such as "fake news," "deep state," and "political correctness." Across the world resentment against immigration, globalization, rising inequality, and a fear of the other all created the fertile conditions for this authoritarian turn.[9] Trump's bluster, his ability to transgress norms, and his willingness to stoke a conspiratorial fringe all drew upon and contributed to the playbook of authoritarian populist leaders.

On January 8, 2023, almost two years to the day after the insurrection, supporters of Jair Bolsonaro in Brazil refused to accept the results of a tight presidential election and marched on government offices in the capital, Brasilia. Bolsonaro had explicitly modeled himself on Trump and was referred to as the Trump of the Tropics. He embraced populist authoritarianism and like Trump he lambasted any criticism of himself as fake news and decried what he referred to as political correctness. Moreover, Bolsonaro also made unsupported claims that his country's election was rigged.

There are many parallels between January 6 in the United States and what happened in Brazil two years later, most notably the promotion of conspiracies by social media. Bolsonaro supporters, like the Capitol rioters, met little resistance on January 8 as the public security forces stood back and let it happen. However, there are major differences. The ransacking of empty federal buildings when the government was not in session was more an articulation of disdain for the electoral process than a grab for power. And perhaps surprisingly given the history of Brazil, there was no support from the military to overturn the close election result. The protestors damaged buildings and furniture more in an authoritarian performative act of resistance than a political coup. One recent study shows how political violence has declined in Brazil because of electronic voting and the rise of programmatic parties, which promise the enactment of specific policies, over clientelist parties that promise resources in return for votes but tend to have close relationships with criminal organizations. The Bolsonaro riots thus look "less like an episode of democratic crisis, and more like turbulence on a long, slow and still incomplete trajectory of democratization."[10] And unlike in the USA, there were immediate consequences for Bolsonaro, who in 2023 was barred by the country's electoral court from political office for the rest of the decade.

The United States has taken a direct hit to its soft power. There are few who saw the scenes on January 6 and now believe that America is a bastion of liberty and democracy. What many people saw was a democracy in crisis, a nation state fractured to the point of violence, the beginning of the end of the American empire. The United States is not alone. Other democracies face similar issues. The UK seems beset by continual political upheaval and constant revelations of political corruption and government incompetence. An unelected prime minister continues to head a deeply unpopular Conservative government. The so-called home of parliamentary democracy faces its own existential crisis. But the United States is different from many other countries in the world, as it plays a significant and unique role in the global economy and the global polity. The growing polarization graphically revealed in the coup and insurrection makes it difficult for the United States to maintain long-term alliances. Under Trump, the country has shown that presidential administrations may quickly pivot away from long-standing agreements. For example, support for Ukraine may not be so forthcoming under a Republican government. In consequence, NATO members may be hesitant to commit too many resources and political capital to a project where American long-term commitment is in doubt. The polarized politics of the domestic level has seeped into the international arena, making the USA an uncertain long-term ally. Other countries question America's stability and its reliability with regard to its geopolitical liabilities. These countries may instead look to other emerging superpowers or to their own regional alliances. In either case, the reputation of the United States as a reliable global power has been devalued in the eyes of many around the world.

To be sure, there's always a danger in freighting a singular event with too many implications. The United States may return to stability, increase its soft power again, and continue to be a major influence in the world for the foreseeable future. There are powerful forces that would seem to guarantee the continued existence of the United States as a global power. Its dynamic economy, its innovative and entrepreneurial culture, its hard-working population, and its commitment to meritocracy are all important factors in giving the United States a continued vitality. However, the insurrection also revealed the depths of the fractures within American society. These are not going away anytime soon. Whether the fractures will rupture, remain taken for granted as part of a new polarized America, or be bridged is an intriguing and hugely significant question not just for the United States but for the whole world.

Consequences

History is a learning process. Events have consequences and consequences have consequences. Let us consider some of the more possibly positive ones.

First, the insurrection highlighted the threat from domestic right-wing groups. Under President Trump the attention of security agencies was focused either on overseas threats or domestic threats from the radical left. Especially since the terrorist attack on September 11, 2001, the rising tide of domestic terrorist groups had gone unnoticed by official authorities. In the two years leading up to the Big Lie the Justice Department and the FBI were focusing on antifa prosecutions and agents felt pressure to uncover left-wing extremists and tended to ignore the far-right threat. There was an exaggeration of the threat from the far left and a downplaying of the threat from the far-right extremists. Counterterrorism agents and resources were focused on the anarchists and thugs of presumed far-left organizations; indeed some resources were shifted away from looking at White supremacist organizations to antifa and others involved in the street protests of the summer of 2020.[11] This led to a normalization of right-wing militia groups. The insurrection has prompted strategic change in national security, with less attention on foreign terrorism and more attention on domestic terrorism, especially the political consequences of a culture of violence that permeates and ultimately poisons the nation.

There is now a more general appreciation of internal dangers. In many cases insurrectionists and demonstrators were called to account by their families, friends, colleagues, and acquaintances, who, recognizing them from videos and clips, reported them to the authorities. It led to a steady procession of people who were arraigned, arrested, and convicted. Some tried to dodge their responsibilities, others accepted blame, and others said that they now realized it was all a dreadful mistake.

The event is difficult to comprehend and encompass in a simple narrative. It was truly dangerous but also farcical. A thin spine of organized violence gave form and coherence to a looser collection of protestors. There were those marching with military precision dressed in paramilitary garb itching to fight. There were also those who broke into the building but then looked mesmerized and befuddled, not sure what to do. This was both a dangerous insurrection and an incoherent mob. We should be wary of reading only one of these messages. The idea that it was a dangerous insurrection ignores its incoherence while the emphasis on an undisciplined mob, described as "just tourists" by some Republican politicians and supporters, ignores the real danger to the Republic. Holding both views at the same time is difficult as most people want a simple, compelling narrative. The very transgression of invading the hallowed civic space created a festival of violence and mayhem. The event was an orgy of populism as well as an attack on democracy.

Second, the attempted coup and the insurrection devalorized Trump in the eyes of many, making him a less potent force. He lost an election, and his persistence with the Big Lie became tedious and whiny, less a call to action and more the ramblings of a fading political star. As Trump loses some of his luster, the Big Lie becomes less important as a mark of ideological purity for Republican politicians. It still resonates with much of the committed base, but as the party needs to widen its support and appeal to more moderate voters in more contestable districts and states, then the commitment to the conspiracy may weaken. In the 2022 midterms many of Trump's picks failed to win.

Trump's hold on the Republican Party continues to exact a loyalty test in the form of confirming the Big Lie and rejecting the legitimacy of Biden's presidency. The longer Biden is president, and the more Trump is beset by legal struggles and scandals, the more Trump's message will fail to move far beyond his bedrock support. He has now moved from the political limelight to the periphery. He still retains enormous influence within the Republican Party but the bully pulpit of the presidency and indeed some social media accounts are no longer available to him. The diminution of his power was most evident in the midterm elections in November 2022, where many election deniers and avid Trump supporters were defeated at the polls. It was an upset result because typically the party in power, in this case the Democrats, tends to lose seats during the midterms, when dissatisfaction with the government is often at its highest.

Throughout the summer of 2022 there was talk of a red wave and the sense that Republicans would sweep back into power by reclaiming the House and the Senate. This did not happen for a couple of reasons. The right-wing majority Supreme Court

decision to overturn *Roe v. Wade* infuriated many people, especially Democrat-leaning voters, throughout the country. There
was also a growing distaste among swing voters for Trump and
his message of bitterness. The election results were surprisingly
close in that the Democrats against the odds held on to power in
the Senate while the Republicans only gained a razor thin majority in the House. An analysis by the right-leaning American
Enterprise Institute was able to quantify Trump's sabotage of
the GOP electoral campaign.[12] Their study found most Trump-
endorsed candidates underperformed. As Trump was beginning
to lose his electoral luster, savvy republican politicians had to
balance off the bedrock support for Trump among Republican
activists in their constituency with a growing sense that Trump
was turning into an electoral obstacle to regaining political
power in Congress.

Trump remains a powerful force, but now mostly in mobilizing the Democratic base and turning off undecided voters.
Trump was turning into what he most feared, a loser. When
Trump announced his second presidential bid on November 15,
2022, soon after the disappointing electoral results, it was met
by lukewarm support from many Republican operatives. The
right-of-center *National Review* had one word on its website in
giant capital letters, *NO*. Even the ever faithful Fox News cut
away from his speech. Meanwhile Trump's decision was silently
welcomed by Democrats, who could see him continuing to
devalue the Republican brand among swing voters. He is not yet
a political irrelevancy, since his ego will continue to undermine
Republican bids for power. He may run again as a strong candidate for the Republican nomination for the presidency. He could
even win. But in the world of politics there is always someone

eager to take your place. As Trump's influence wanes, new contenders will emerge. Political ambition is a never-ending source of political change.

Third, there is now a more critical eye cast on the role of social media. This more informed awareness will have to work against the enormous power and influence of social media and powerful media companies, but there is a growing consensus that some form of regulation is required to rein in the uncontrolled realm of proliferating lies and conspiracies. It is of course a difficult balance to both encourage and regulate free speech in the interests of social peace and stability. It is an awkward, uneasy, and difficult conversation to have. The insurrection gave visual testimony to the need for some form of renewed conversation about the regulation of social media and the blatant political partisanship masquerading as news.

Fourth, there is a reaction to Trump's attempted cognitive capture. Trump lied and lied often. His lies were repeated and reinforced by a superstructure of mendacity of cabinet ministers, celebrities, newscasters, friends, and business associates, and in the early years by a supine press and spineless media. In contrast, when Donald Trump announced his candidacy for the 2024 presidential election, the *Washington Post* led with the headline, "Trump Who as President Fomented an Insurrection Says He Is Running Again." The article continued: "twice-impeached former president has been eager to declare his candidacy hoping to get ahead of likely rivals and potential criminal charges."[13] It was a sign of the times; there was no longer the vapid middle-of-the-road political discussion of, "on the one hand, but on the other." Trump's mendacity led to this major revision of how political news and events should be covered and reported. By 2022, Trump was not given the pass he was afforded in his run-up in 2015 or the endless CNN coverage of his every speech in his first presidential campaign. American media, or at least some of them, had learned their lesson: to passively assist demagogues is a form of demagoguery itself. A chastened mass media now looks more critically at Trump, his claims, and his wild assertions. It is now a harder, gimlet-eyed view of a man who once was president and unleashed forces that threatened democracy itself. It may even represent a press better able to handle lies and falsehoods. This may lead to more polarization if some choose to see this more critical stance as fake news, but if we are to avoid living in a post-truth United States, then truth, in all its imprecision and uncertainty, needs to be the primary goal of news reporting and media coverage.

Finally, on a more positive note, we can look forward, perhaps, to Trump fading from view as his political capital is expended and his legal worries mount. He will be abandoned by the political leadership of the Republican Party. He served his purpose; he gained the presidency and promoted many Republican objectives. He transformed the Supreme Court with the selection of right-wing hacks. He unleashed very dark forces in the American body politic that will continue to challenge the nation. But he also generated real fear. The presidency of Donald Trump was a chastening experience. Many in the country were truly shocked at his relatively easy undermining of traditional political norms. He re-energized a democratic impulse, raised a more critical awareness among mainstream media, and highlighted the dangers of conspiracy theories and of insurrectionary forces in the USA. There is both a danger in the forces that Trump unleashed but also, countering that, a renewed sense of the need to protect what we now realize is a vulnerable democracy. In the United

States democracy had long been taken for granted, assumed as an eternal verity. Trump's attempt to undermine it made us more aware of its fragility. The fact that Trump could achieve such high office reminded us that the greatest threats to democracy come from within. Trump's greatest and positive legacy is a reawakening among the American public that democracy in the United States is not a given, it is not guaranteed by the founders, by the Constitution, or by the weight of the past. It is a system that can at certain times and by certain people be disturbingly easy to erode and undermine. He reminded us all that democracy in America, like democracies everywhere, has to be protected and maintained, that democracy is not an achieved destination but an ongoing project. The USA is clearly not a failed state. Not yet anyway. But the insurrection was a reminder that democracy needs to tended, nurtured, and defended because at times it also has the delicate gossamer architecture of a spider web, easily ripped apart and difficult to reassemble.

A Slide into Authoritarianism?

Does Trump, his presidency, and the insurrection mark an inflection point for a dangerous permanent slide into authoritarianism? It was Tom Wolfe who remarked that "the dark night of fascism is always descending in the United States and yet lands only in Europe."[14] While the first part of the famous quote is perhaps true, the second is less assured. There have always been darkening forces in the body politic. Conspiracy theories seem to be part of the country's political DNA so we should be careful of assigning too much special significance to this moment. And yet, I think we should. We are in a significant political moment in the Republic.

Social media have made the transmission of conspiracy theories so much easier while social and economic dislocations have created a fertile environment for their eager acceptance. And now one of the only two main parties, the Republican Party, is sliding into an anti-democratic, populist authoritarianism that may put the democratic experiment of America in serious jeopardy.

Trump was an authoritarian but an incompetent one. The next time we may not be so lucky. There are, of course, too many competing centers of power for an easy slide into a centralized authoritarianism. More likely is the emergence of a cultural and political authoritarianism at the state level and sometimes at the federal level, punctuated by resistances and occasional overturnings. The 2020 presidential election outcome galvanized the poltical right and social conservatives. The last few years have seen more aggressively interventionist state legislatures proposing bans on abortion, limiting free speech, curtailing the teaching of u.s. history, and banning books. A Supreme Court packed with illiberal ideologues provides some support and little resistance to this scary rightward shift. These are not actions that suggest we are moving toward a more open and vigorous democracy. We are moving down a darker path.

In their comparative framework the political scientists Steven Levitsky and Daniel Ziblatt argue that democracies are kept alive by adherence to established norms, gatekeeping, and biparti-san alliances.[15] The election of an authoritarian leader can pose a democratic challenge especially if and when norms are trans-gressed, gatekeeping functions such as an independent judiciary or free press slide into toadyism, and there is hyperpartisanship. Authoritarian leaders exploit the weaknesses in the system to solidify their grip. Democracies rarely die in flames; they collapse from slow strangulation. In the United States there is a free press and an independent judiciary, but under Trump the USA was still taken to the edge of political unconsciousness. We have not yet retreated back to safety.

Political scientist Barbara F. Walter suggests that civil wars take place against a background of eroding political institutions, extreme racial-ethnic factionalization, and the capacity of prominent leaders to foment violence.[16] Sound familiar? The extreme right-wing groups constitute a threat, but arguably not a major one, as there is such an asymmetry between their limited power and the forces of the state, especially the police and military. They are unlikely to obtain much traction now that security forces and the military–industrial–security complex are pivoting away from a fear of foreign terrorism toward a recognition of the domestic threat posed by right-wing militia groups with violent ideologies. To concentrate on the right-wing extremists or talk of a second civil war is to miss the point. The real threat is not from a bunch of losers in tactical gear spouting wild conspiracies. The biggest threat is from established leaders, certain mainstream media such as Fox News, Republican politicians, and a Republican base that refuses to accept a lost election. Subsequent defeats will be seen increasingly as the result of some flawed process at best and the deep state at worst. The long-term danger is of an asymmetrical polarization, with the Republican Party falling off the cliff into crazy conspiracy land, a growing legitimacy crisis, a deepening sense that violence is justified, and the increasing feeling among American citizens that they are losing their country. The United States is awash in guns, and many people increasingly believe in the sanctity of using them to fight against the government.

We should also be wary of concentrating too much on Trump. He was as much a symptom as a cause. He revealed some of the frailties of the American experiment against a background of social and economic tension and extreme political polarizations including but not limited to an archaic electoral system, too long a gap between election result and the installation of a new administration, and a lack of clarity about the confirmation of a president. Trump was perhaps the first president in modern times who fully exploited these ambiguities to resist being voted from office. It is therefore fair to say that future elected officials could do the same or worse, exploiting the shortcomings of the system and abusing the constitutional opportunities for mayhem.

Trump gave the United States one of its greatest stress tests. A pessimistic view of America sees the country sliding into chaos, decay, violence, and eventual collapse. Some see the system as breaking up like some galactic supernova. But there is another scenario. It was T. S. Eliot who foretold the world will end not with a bang but a whimper. The United States is at danger of a steady erosion from the inside—at times slowly, sometimes quickly, at other times imperceptibly. Much needed legislation will fall by the wayside, politics will be so demeaned that politicians and politics will no longer be seen as a vehicle for social improvement. As we lose the sense that governments can work for the greater good, we will inhabit a world of hyperpartisan and polarized communities, a country of simmering resentment, boiling anger, and growing political polarization. If anything, things may get worse. An increasing weaponization of government will mean administrations could spend most of their time seeking to criminalize the actions of their predecessors. In such a fetid atmosphere there seems little hope of a more bipartisan politics emerging. Polarization may indeed get worse, and government could degenerate from passing important and much-needed legislation for the general welfare to simply abusing power to settle political scores.

The state will not collapse. Life will go on. The United States will survive. It is so big and rich that, like a trust-fund baby, it will have enough to get by on for quite a while. The decline may not be as dramatic as the civil war imagined by some commentators. It could be a slow arc of decline and who can say what a post-democratic, post-optimistic, post-truth America will look like?

* * *

Let me conclude by again recalling the advice of the very first president. In his farewell address on September 19, 1796, George Washington pleaded for a united country. He warned against "cunning ambitious and unprincipled men" and a destructive partisan force that "agitates the community with ill-founded jealousies and false alarms, kindles the animosity of one part against another, foments occasionally riot and insurrection."

References

Preface

1 "Transcript of Trump's Speech at Rally before U.S. Capitol Riot," *AP News*, https://apnews.com, January 13, 2021.

1 From the Small Lie to the Big Lie

1 M. Ruane, "DC's Inauguration Head Count: 1.8 million," *Washington Post*, www.washingtonpost.com, January 20, 2009.

2 "Full Text: 2017 Donald Trump Inauguration Speech Transcript," *Politico*, www.politico.com, January 20, 2017.

3 "Conway: Press Secretary Gave 'Alternative Facts'," *NBC*, www.nbcnews.com, January 22, 2017.

4 Friedrich Nietzche, *Will to Power* [1901], trans. Walter Kaufmann (New York, 1968): "facts is precisely what there is not, only interpretations," p. 60.

5 G. Kessler, S. Rizzo, and M. Kelly, "Trump's False or Misleading Claims Total 30,573 over 4 Years," *Washington Post*, www.washingtonpost.com, January 24, 2021.

6 Jake Tapper, "How to Interview Donald Trump," *New York Public Radio*, www.wnycstudios.org, June 10, 2016.

7 Ashley Parker and Josh Dawsey, "Trump's Cable Cabinet: New Texts Reveal the Influence of Fox Hosts on Previous White House," *Washington Post*, www.washingtonpost.com, January 9, 2022.

8 The personality psychologist Dan McAdams asserts that Trump could lie so easily and so often because he had no sense of himself, he had no autobiographical ground truth. He lives solely in the emotional moment. "Trump is not introspective, retrospective or prospective. There is no depth; there is no past; there is no future."

D. McAdams, *The Strange Case of Donald J. Trump: A Psychological Reckoning* (New York, 2020), p. 4.

9 Donald Trump, *The Art of the Deal* (New York, 1987). For the views of the ghost writer, Tony Schwartz, see J. Mayer, "Donald Trump's Ghost Writer Tells All," *New Yorker*, www.newyorker.com, 7 July, 2016.

10 Nick Penzenstadler and Steve Reilly, "Donald Trump: Three Decades, 4,095 lawsuits," *USA Today*, www.usatoday.com, 2018.

11 E. Paravati et al., "More Than Just a Tweet: The Unconscious Impact of Forming Parasocial Relationships through Social Media," *Psychology of Consciousness: Theory, Research, and Practice*, VII (2020), pp. 388–403; E. Paravati et al., "From Apprentice to President: The Role of Parasocial Connection in the Election of Donald Trump," *Social Psychological and Personality Science*, IX (2018), pp. 299–307.

12 W. J. Brady et al., "Emotion Shapes the Diffusion of Moralized Content in Social Networks," *Proceedings of the National Academy of Sciences*, CXIV (2018), pp. 7313–18; W. J. Brady et al., "An Ideological Asymmetry in the Diffusion of Moralized Content on Social Media among Political Leaders," *Journal of Experimental Psychology: General*, CXLVIII (2019), p. 1802: W. J. Brady, A. P. Gantman, and J. J. Van Bavel, "Attentional Capture Helps Explain Why Moral and Emotional Content Go Viral," *Journal of Experimental Psychology: General*, CXLIX (2020), pp. 746–56.

13 John Rennie Short, "What to Do about Trump Fatigue Syndrome," *Hippo Reads*, http://hipporeads.com, 2017.

14 Dylan Matthews, "The F Word," *Vox*, www.vox.com, January 14, 2021. For a more considered critical take, see Geoff Eley, "Is Trump a Fascist?" *Historians for Peace and Democracy*, https://historiansforpeace.org, 2018.

15 F. Hill, *There Is Nothing for You Here* (Boston, MA, and New York, 2021).

16 E. Fromm, *Escape from Freedom* (New York, 1941). See also J. W. Dean and B. Altemeyer, *Authoritarian Nightmare: Trump and His Followers* (New York, 2020); D. Kellner, "Donald Trump as Authoritarian Populist: A Frommian Analysis," in *Critical Theory and Authoritarian Populism*, ed. J. Morelock (London, 2018), pp. 71–82; K. Larres, "Donald J. Trump: The Authoritarian Style in American Politics," in *Dictators and Autocrats*, ed. K. Larres (London, 2021),

References

pp. 204–31; M. C. MacWilliams, "Who Decides When the Party Doesn't? Authoritarian Voters and the Rise of Donald Trump," *PS: Political Science and Politics*, XLIX (2016), pp. 716–21.

17 Dan P. McAdams, "The Mind of Donald Trump," *The Atlantic*, www.theatlantic.com, June 15, 2016.

18 A. Nai, F. Martínez i Coma, and J. Maier, "Donald Trump, Populism, and the Age of Extremes: Comparing the Personality Traits and Campaigning Styles of Trump and Other Leaders Worldwide," *Presidential Studies Quarterly*, XLIX (2019), pp. 609–43.

19 The accounts range from the contextual studies to the insider accounts, family gossip, and more formal interviews. A sample: P. Baker and S. Glasser, *The Divider: Trump in the White House, 2017–2021* (New York, 2022); J. Bolton, *The Room Where It Happened: A White House Memoir* (New York, 2020); Maggie Haberman, *Confidence Man: The Making of Donald Trump and the Breaking of America* (New York, 2022); A. Immelman and A. M. Griebie, "The Personality Profile and Leadership Style of U.S. President Donald J. Trump in Office," *Digital Commons*, https://digitalcommons. csbsju.edu, 2020; B. Lee et al., *The Dangerous Case of Donald Trump* (New York, 2019); C. Lozada, *What Were We Thinking: A Brief Intellectual History of the Trump Era* (New York, 2020); D. McAdams, *The Strange Case of Donald J. Trump: A Psychological Reckoning* (New York, 2020); M. Maccoby and K. Fuchsman, *Psychoanalytic and Historical Perspectives on the Leadership of Donald Trump: Narcissism and Marketing in an Age of Anxiety and Distrust* (New York, 2020); Nai, Martínez i Coma, and Maier, "Donald Trump, Populism, and the Age of Extremes"; A. Scaramucci, *Trump: The Blue Collar President* (New York, 2018); C. Thorpe, "The Carnival King of Capital," *Fast Capitalism*, XVII (2020); M. L. Trump, *Too Much and Never Enough* (New York, 2020); B. Woodward, *Fear: Trump in The White House* (New York, 2018); B. Woodward, *Rage* (New York, 2020); M. Wolff, *Fire and Fury: Inside The White House* (New York, 2018); J. K. Wilson, *Trump Unveiled: Exposing the Bigoted Billionaire* (New York, 2016).

20 The transactional relationship of the outer court was soon revealed after January 6 and Trump's fall from power. William Barr was appointed attorney general by Trump and did his bidding, including interfering with a critical report on Trump's Russian connections. Barr later turned on his former boss in a 2022 self-serving memoir,

One Damn Thing After Another, that was a transparent attempt by Barr to salvage his damaged reputation. Barr was slow off the mark to distance himself compared to Elaine Chao. She served as transportation secretary in the Trump Administration from 2017 to 2021. Her appointment, one of many she has had including as secretary of labor (2001–9), is less a function of her abilities than her connections. She is the wife of Republican Senate leader Mitch McConnell. Her cabinet appointments were a failsafe way for Republican presidents to ingratiate themselves with her powerful husband. She worked at Transportation during the entire Trump presidency and only resigned on January 7, 2022, one day after the insurrection. It was less an act of political courage, as it was mere days before she would have been forced to leave anyway, and more a confirmation that she and her husband no longer needed Trump now that he was out of power.

21 Igor Bobic, "Trump Invites His Employees to Praise Him During Cabinet Meeting," *Huffington Post*, www.youtube.com, June 12, 2017.

22 J. Goldberg, "James Mattis Denounces President Trump, Describes Him as a Threat to the Constitution," *The Atlantic*, www.theatlantic.com, June 3, 2020.

23 The two polls are available here: https://news.gallup.com/poll/203198/presidential-approval-ratings-donald-trump.aspx and https://projects.fivethirtyeight.com/trump-approval-ratings, both accessed February 20, 2023.

24 S. Zito, "Taking Trump Seriously, Not Literally," *The Atlantic*, www.theatlantic.com, September 23, 2016.

25 I am grateful to my friend Maureen Hays-Mitchell for writing down the words on the signs at the Women's March in Washington.

26 David Floyd, "Explaining the Trump Tax Reform Plan," *Investopedia*, www.investopedia.com, January 23, 2023.

27 J. Boehner, *On The House: A Washington Memoir* (New York, 2021).

28 T. Skocpol and V. Williamson, *The Tea Party and the Remaking of Republican Conservatism* (New York, 2016); J. E. Zelizer, *Burning Down the House: Newt Gingrich, The Fall of a Speaker and the Rise of the New Republican Party* (New York, 2020).

29 Allan Sloan and Cezary Podkul, "Donald Trump Built a National Debt so Big (Even before the Pandemic) that it'll Weigh Down the Economy for Years," *ProPublica*, www.propublica.org, January 14, 2021.

30 S. Benen, *The Imposters: How Republicans Quit Governing and Seized American Politics* (New York, 2020).

31 J. S. Hacker and P. Pierson, *Let Them Eat Tweets: How the Right Rules in an Age of Extreme Inequality* (New York, 2020).

32 R. Draper, *Weapons of Mass Delusion: When the Republican Party Lost Its Mind* (New York, 2020).

2 Losing Trust in Government

1 D. Ariely, *The Honest Truth about Dishonesty* (New York, 2012).

2 "President Obama at White House Correspondents Dinner," *YouTube*, www.youtube.com, May 1, 2011.

3 Adam Gopnik, "Trump and Obama: A Night to Remember," *New Yorker*, www.newyorker.com, September 12, 2015; R. Roberts, "I Sat Next to Donald Trump at the Infamous 2011 White House Correspondents Dinner," *Washington Post*, www.washingtonpost.com, April 28, 2016.

4 J. Habermas, *Legitimation Crisis* (London, 1976).

5 The Rasmussen Polls: "35% Say u.s. Heading in Right Direction," *Rasmussen Reports*, www.rasmussenreports.com, February 13, 2023; "What They Told Us: Reviewing Last Week's Key Polls," *Rasmussen Reports*, www.rasmussenreports.com, February 11, 2023; The Gallup Poll: "Confidence in Institutions," *Gallup*, https://news.gallup.com, July 5, 2022; The Pew Research Center Poll: "Trust in Government: 1958–2015," *Pew Research Center*, www.pewresearch.org, November 23, 2015.

6 "First Inaugural Address of Ronald Reagan," *The Avalon Project*, https://avalon.law.yale.edu.

7 See the revealing title of an excellent Roosevelt biography: H. W. Brands, *Traitor to His Class: The Privileged Life and Radical Presidency of Franklin Delano Roosevelt* (New York, 2009).

8 "The Jan. 6 Capitol Attacks Offer a Reminder—Distrust in Government Has Long Been Part of Republicans' Playbook," *The Conversation*, https://theconversation.com, February 9, 2022.

9 A. Fried and D. B. Harris, *How Conservatives Weaponized Distrust from Goldwater to Trump* (New York, 2021).

10 S. Mettler, *The Submerged State: How Invisible Government Policies Undermine American Democracy* (Chicago, IL, 2012).

11 G. Gerstle, *The Rise and Fall of Neoliberalism: The Collapse of an Economic Order* (New York, 2022).

12 S. Johnson, "The Quiet Coup," *The Atlantic*, www.theatlantic.com, May 2009.

13 L. Mishel, E. Gould, and J. Bivens, "Wage Stagnation in Nine Charts," *Economic Policy Institute*, www.epi.org, 2015.

14 A. Case and A. Deaton, *Deaths of Despair and the Future of Capitalism* (Princeton, NJ, 2020).

15 Elise Gould, "Higher Returns on Education Can't Explain Growing Wage Inequality," *Economic Policy Institute*, www.epi.org, March 15, 2019.

16 Paul Specht, "Fact Check: How Many Student Loan Borrowers Failed to Finish College?" *WRAL* News, www.wral.com, February 15, 2021.

17 I. Berlin, *Four Essays on Liberty* (Oxford, 1969).

18 A. R. Hochschild, *Strangers in Their Own Land: Anger and Mourning on the American Right* (New York, 2016).

19 Alec Tyson and Shiva Maniam, "Behind Trump's Victory: Divisions by Race, Gender, Education," *Pew Research Center*, www.pewresearch.org, November 9, 2016.

20 Diane Katz, "The Decline of the American Labor Union," https://www.gisreportsonline.com, April 28, 2023.

21 Case and Deaton, *Deaths of Despair and the Future of Capitalism*. See also D. Leonhardt and S. A. Thompson, "How Working-Class Life Is Killing Americans, in Charts," *New York Times*, www.nytimes.com, March 6, 2020; J. C. Williams, *White Working Class* (Boston, MA, 2020).

22 See K. Payne, *The Broken Ladder: How Inequality Affects the Way We Think, Live and Die* (New York, 2017).

23 T. Mann and N. J. Ornstein, *It's Even Worse Than It Was* (New York, 2015).

24 A. Maxwell and T. Shields, *The Long Southern Strategy: How Chasing White Voters in the South Changed American Politics* (New York, 2019).

25 Sara Burnett, "AP-NORC Poll: Most in U.S. Say They Want Strict Gun Control," *AP News*, https://apnews.com, August 23, 2022.

26 D. Mutz, "Status Threat, Not Economic Hardship, Explains the 2016 Presidential Vote," *Proceedings of the National Academy of Sciences*, CXV/19 (2017).

27 I draw heavily on my previous work, John Rennie Short, "Globalization and Its Discontents," *The Conversation*, https://theconversation.com, November 28, 2016.

28 J. Bivens, "Using Standard Models to Benchmark the Costs of Globalization for American Workers without a College Degree," *Economic Policy Institute*, www.epi.org, March 22, 2013.

3 A Flawed Democracy

1 "A New Low for Global Democracy," *The Economist*, www.economist.com, February 9, 2022.

2 J. Madison, "Federalist Papers No. 10," *Bill of Rights Institute*, https://billofrightsinstitute.org, 1787.

3 B. Tau and J. Bykowicz, "FBI Probes Defense Contractor's Contributions to Sen. Susan Collins," *Wall Street Journal*, www.wsj.com, May 18, 2021.

4 Benjamin Page, "How Money Corrupts American Politics," www.scholars.org, June 19, 2013.

5 Kristen Bialik, "State of the Union 2018: Americans' Views on Key Issues Facing the Nation," *Pew Research Center*, www.pewresearch.org, January 29, 2018.

6 Kevin McMahon, "Is the Supreme Court's Legitimacy Undermined in a Polarized Age?" *The Conversation*, https://theconversation.com, October 10, 2018.

7 The total number of representatives in the House is limited to 435.

8 "America's Electoral System Gives the Republicans Advantages over Democrats," *The Economist*, www.economist.com, July 12, 2018.

9 These are voters who identify themselves as Jewish voters, as opposed to Jews who vote but do not consider themselves Jewish voters.

10 J. R. Short, "Four Reasons Gerrymandering Is Getting Worse," *The Conversation*, https://theconversation.com, October 29, 2018.

11 D. Daley, "The Secret Files of the Master of Modern Republican Gerrymandering," *New Yorker*, www.newyorker.com, September 6, 2019.

12 M. Li, "Extreme Maps," www.brennancenter.org, May 9, 2017.

13 J. M. Burns, *Packing the Court* (New York, 2009), p. 93.

14 For U.S. Census data on Alabama and Shelby County, see www.census.gov, accessed August 31, 2023; J. R. Short, "The Supreme Court, the Voting Rights Act and Competing National

Imaginaries of the USA," *Territory, Politics, Governance*, 2 (2014), pp. 94–108.

15 "The Myth of Voter Fraud," *Brennan Center for Justice*, www.brennancenter.org, 2022.

16 J. R. Short, "The Legitimation Crisis in the USA: Why Have Americans Lost Trust in Government?" *The Conversation*, https://theconversation.com, October 21, 2016.

4 Conspiracy and the Politics of Outrage

1 There is a vast literature. See M. Butter, "Conspiracy Theories in American History," in *Routledge Handbook of Conspiracy Theories*, ed. M. Butter and P. Knight (London, 2020), pp. 648–59; P. Knight, *Conspiracy Theories in American History: An Encyclopedia* (Santa Barbara, CA, 2003). For the contemporary period see M. Barkun, *A Culture of Conspiracy: Apocalyptic Visions in Contemporary America*, 2nd edn (Berkeley and Los Angeles, CA, 2013); R. A. Goldberg, *"Enemies Within": The Culture of Conspiracy in Modern America* (New Haven, CT, 2001); P. Knight, *Conspiracy Nation: The Politics of Paranoia in Postwar America* (New York, 2002); and K. S. Olmsted, *Real Enemies: Conspiracy Theories and American Democracy, World War I to 9/11* (Oxford, 2019).

2 R. Hofstadter, "The Paranoid Style in American Politics," *Harper's Bazaar*, November 1964, available at https://harpers.org.

3 A. Spark, "Conjuring Order: The New World Order and Conspiracy Theories of Globalization," *Sociological Review*, XLVIII (2000), pp. 46–62.

4 T. Egan, "Politics: A New Populist," *New York Times*, www.nytimes.com, January 15, 1996.

5 M. Barkun, *Millennialism and Violence* (London, 1996).

6 N. Sheehan et al., *The Pentagon Papers: The Secret History of the Vietnam War* (New York, 2017); C. Whitlock, *The Afghanistan Papers: A Secret History of the War* (New York, 2021).

7 M. Barkun, "Conspiracy Theories as Stigmatized Knowledge," *Diogenes*, LXII (2015), pp. 114–20.

8 M. Bender, *Frankly, We Did Win This Election* (New York and Boston, MA, 2021).

9 X. Márquez, "The Mechanisms of Cult Production: An Overview," in *Ruler Personality Cults from Empires to Nation-States*

and Beyond: Symbolic Patterns and Interactional Dynamics, ed.
K. Postoutenko and D. Stephanov (Oxford and New York, 2020),
pp. 21–45.

10   R. Igienik, S. Keeter, and Hannah Hartig, "Behind Biden's 2020
Victory," *Pew Research Center*, www.pewresearch.org, June 30, 2021.

11   See M. Margolis, *From Politics to the Pews: How Partisanship and the
Political Environment Shape Religious Identity* (Chicago, IL, 2018).

12   See K. Kobes Du Mez, *Jesus and John Wayne: How White Evangelicals
Corrupted a Faith and Fractured a Nation* (New York, 2020).

13   See P. S. Gorski and S. L. Perry, *The Flag and the Cross: White
Christian Nationalism and the Threat to Democracy* (New York, 2022).

14   A. Snow, "1 in 3 Fear Immigrants Influence U.S. Elections: AP-NPRC
Poll," *AP News*, https://apnews.com, May 10, 2022.

15   See also A. L. Whitehead and S. Perry, *Taking America Back for God:
Christian Nationalism in the United States* (New York, 2020).

16   M. Barkun, "Donald Trump and the Myth of the Deep State," in
Exposing the Right and Fighting for Democracy, ed. P. Chamberlin
et al. (London, 2021), pp. 114–20; Barkun, "Conspiracy Theories
as Stigmatized Knowledge," pp. 3–4. See also M. Barkun,
"President Trump and the 'Fringe'," *Terrorism and Political
Violence*, XXIX (2017), pp. 437–43; K. Olmsted, "Fringe Paranoia
Goes Mainstream," *Modern American History*, I (2018),
pp. 243–6.

17   See P. A. Turner, *I Heard It Through the Grapevine: Rumor in
African-American Culture* (Berkeley and Los Angeles, CA, 1993).

18   Quote from J. S. Huntington, *Far-Right Vanguard: The Radical
Roots of Modern Conservatism* (Philadelphia, PA, 2021), p. 218.
For other discussions of this rightward shift see R. Perlstein,
Reaganland: America's Right Turn, 1976–1980 (New York, 2020);
and N. Hemmer's *Partisans: The Conservative Revolutionaries
Who Remade American Politics in the 1990s* (New York, 2022) and
*Messengers of the Right: Conservative Media and the Transformation
of American Politics* (Philadelphia, PA, 2016).

19   See P. Matzko, *The Radio Right: How a Band of Broadcasters Took
on the Federal Government and Built the Conservative Movement*
(New York, 2020).

20   B. Rosenwald, *Talk Radio: How an Industry Took over a Political
Party that Took over the United States* (Cambridge, 2019).

21   See Hemmer, *The Conservative Revolutionaries*.

22 The parents of Sandy Hook victims filed a lawsuit against Jones who, in his defense, claimed he had psychosis. He was eventually banned from most social media platforms by 2020 and filed for bankruptcy in 2022.

23 "InfoWars: Alex Jones Interviews Donald Trump – December 2, 2015," *YouTube*, www.youtube.com, November 3, 2017.

24 For more on the strange worlds of Jones, Trump, and Infowars see A. Merlan, *Republic of Lies: American Conspiracy Theorists and Their Surprising Rise to Power* (New York, 2019); E. Williamson, *Sandy Hook: An American Tragedy and the Battle for Truth* (New York, 2022).

25 Section 230 of the 1996 Communications Decency Act. Under this law social media companies can set their own standards for content. They do not bear any legal liability for the content or any social responsibility to ensure it is fair and accurate.

26 A. Robb, "'Pizzagate': Anatomy of a Fake News Scandal," *Rolling Stone*, www.rollingstone.com, November 16, 2017.

27 J. Kline, "C. G. Jung and Norman Cohn Explain Pizzagate: The Archetypal Dimension of a Conspiracy Theory," *Psychological Perspectives*, LX (2017), pp. 186–95.

28 N. Cohn, *Europe's Inner Demons: The Demonization of Christians in Medieval Christendom* (Chicago, IL, 1993).

29 See R. Beck, *We Believe the Children: A Moral Panic in the 1980s* (New York, 2015).

30 A. Breland, "Why Are Right-Wing Conspiracies So Obsessed with Pedophilia?" *Mother Jones*, www.motherjones.com, July/August 2019.

31 See, for example, A. Cornwall and Nancy Lindisfarne, *Dislocating Masculinity*, 2nd edn (London, 2016).

32 Among the many studies that buttress this remark, see E. Klein, *Why We're Polarized* (New York, 2020); E. Osnos, *Wildland: The Making of America's Fury* (New York, 2021); T. K. Vescio and N. E. Schermerhorn, "Hegemonic Masculinity Predicts 2016 and 2020 Voting and Candidate Evaluations," *Proceedings of the National Academy of Sciences*, CXVIII/2 (2021); J. C. Williams, *White Working Class: Overcoming Class Cluelessness in America* (Boston, MA, 2017).

33 S. M. Lipset, *American Exceptionalism: A Double-Edged Sword* (New York, 1996).

34 There is an alternative story of the American Revolution, one that stresses a decade of nonviolent resistance struggles. That this story

receives so little attention is highly illuminating about the chosen origin myth of the United States. See Benjamin Naimark-Rowse, "u.s. Independence Won by Nonviolent Resistance before the War," *PopularResistance.org*, https://popularresistance.org, July 2, 2017.

35 Meryl Kornfield and Mariana Alfaro, "1 in 3 Americans Say Violence Against Government Can Be Justified, Citing Fears of Political Schism, Pandemic," *Washington Post*, www.washingtonpost.com, January 1, 2022.

36 B. Stelter, *Hoax: Donald Trump, Fox News and the Dangerous Distortion of the Truth* (New York, 2020).

37 In the poll taken just before the 2020 election, at least half of Donald Trump supporters agreed with the assertion that top Democrats are involved in child sex-trafficking rings. Graeme Bruce, "Half of Trump's Supporters Think Top Democrats Are Involved in Child Sex-Trafficking," *YouGovAmerica*, https://today.yougov.com, October 20, 2020.

38 Noah Caldwell et al., "America's Satanic Panic Returns—This Time through QAnon," *NPR*, www.npr.org, May 18, 2021.

39 George Will, "Donald Trump and Boris Johnson Have Much in Common, with One Vital, Deflating Difference," *Washington Post*, www.washingtonpost.com, February 2, 2022.

5 The Year Before: Pandemic and the Crises of Policing

1 In 2022 and for six years previously, the right-of-center *Economist* ranked the United States as a flawed democracy. It was demoted from a full democracy in 2016. In 2022 the usa placed 26th out of 167 countries. The United States is just one country experiencing less democracy as the world experiences a mounting democratic deficit. See "Democracy Index 2020: In Sickness and in Health?" *Economist Intelligence*, www.eiu.com.

2 B. Woodward, *Rage* (New York, 2020), pp. xiii–xv.

3 In all of 2020, 385,000 Americans died from the disease. At the time of writing, in early 2022, the total was closing in on 1 million.

4 Y. Abutaleb and D. Paletta, *Nightmare Scenarios: Inside the Trump Administration's Response to the Pandemic that Changed History* (New York, 2021); C. Leonning and P. Rucker, *I Alone Can Fix It:*

Donald J. Trump's Catastrophic Final Year (New York, 2021); J. R. Short, *Stress Testing the USA* (New York, 2021).

5 A. de Tocqueville, *Democracy in America* [1835–40], trans. J. P Mayer (New York, 2006).

6 B. L. Stanley et al., "Collective Emotion during Collective Trauma: A Metaphor Analysis of the COVID-19 Pandemic," *Qualitative Health Research*, XXXI (2021), pp. 1890–903; E. B. Fisher et al., "COVID-19, Stress, Trauma, and Peer Support—Observations from the Field," *Translational Behavioral Medicine*, 10 (2020), pp. 503–5.

7 Kristian Blickle, "Pandemics Change Cities: Municipal Spending and Voter Extremism in Germany, 1918–1933," *Federal Reserve Board of New York Staff Report* 921 (2020).

8 S. Sontag, *AIDS and Its Metaphors* (New York, 1989).

9 G. Davies, E. Wu, and R. Frank, "A Witch's Brew of Grievances: The Potential Effects of COVID-19 on Radicalization to Violent Extremism," *Studies in Conflict and Terrorism* (2021), pp. 1–24; W. Avis, "The COVID-19 Pandemic and Response on Violent Extremist Recruitment and Radicalisation," *HelpDesk*, https://opendocs.ids.ac.uk, May 4, 2020.

10 N. Bogel-Burroughs, S. Dewan, and K. Gray, "FBI Says Michigan Anti-Government Group Plotted to Kidnap Gov. Gretchen Whitmer," *New York Times*, www.nytimes.com, October 8, 2022; M. Smith, "Jury Convicts Men of Supporting Plot to Kidnap Michigan Governor," *New York Times*, www.nytimes.com, October 26, 2022.

11 T.-N. Coates, *Between the World and Me* (New York, 2015), p. 71.

12 Samuel Johnson, *Taxation No Tyranny* (orig. London, 1775), www.samueljohnson.com/tnt.html.

13 J. Zauzmer, A. Blanco, and L. Dominguez, "More than 1,800 Congressmen Once Enslaved Black People. This Is Who They Were, and How They Shaped the Nation," *Washington Post*, www.washingtonpost.com, January 10, 2022.

14 Coates, *Between the World and Me*, p. 7.

15 J. Leovy, *Ghettoside: A True Story of Murder in America* (New York, 2015).

16 E. Hinton, *America on Fire: The Untold History of Police Violence and Black Rebellion Since the 1960s* (New York, 2021).

17 "Gun Violence in the U.S. and What the Statistics Tell Us," *BBC News*, www.bbc.com; M. Delisa, "What Other Countries Show

Us about America's Gun Violence Epidemic," *ABC News*, https://
abcnews.go, November 5, 2021; K. Fox et al., "How U.S. Gun
Culture Stacks Up with the World," *CNN*, www.cnn.com,
January 23, 2023.

18 N. Aizenman, "Gun Violence Deaths: How the U.S. Compares
with the Rest of the World," *NPR*, www.npr.org, January 24, 2023.

19 J. J. Van der Weele, M. P. Flynn, and R. J. Van der Wolk, "Broken
Window Effect," *Encyclopedia of Law and Economics* (2017),
www.joelvanderweele.eu, accessed July 6, 2023.

20 R. Tan, "There's a Reason It's Hard to Discipline Police. It
Starts with the Bill of Rights 40 Years Ago," *Washington Post*,
www.washingtonpost.com, August 19, 2020.

21 C. Boudin, "The Police Answer to Us. What Will We Do About
It?" *New York Times*, www.nytimes.com, July 27, 2020.

22 Richard Fausset, "What We Know about the Shooting Death
of Ahmaud Arbery," *New York Times*, www.nytimes.com, August 8,
2022.

23 T. Brannstrom, "Alleged Police Misconduct Cost Yonkers, NY,
Millions. The Complaints Kept Coming," *National Public Radio*,
www.npr.org, July 31, 2022.

24 R. Klemko, "Much of America Wants Policing to Change but these
Self-Proclaimed Experts Tell Officers They're Doing Just Fine,"
Washington Post, www.washingtonpost.com, January 26, 2022.

25 "United States Department of Justice Civil Rights Division,"
Investigation of the Ferguson Police, www.justice.gov, March 4, 2015.

26 But, despite the oft-made claims, not the most dangerous
occupation in the country. It ranks around 22nd.

27 See the *Washington Post* database on police shooting and civilian
deaths, www.washingtonpost.com/graphics/investigations/police-
shootings-database, accessed August 1, 2023.

28 E. Pierson et al., "A Large-Scale Analysis of Racial Disparities in
Police Stops across the United States," *Nature Human Behaviour*,
4 (2020), pp. 736–45.

29 S. A. Seo, *Policing the Open Road: How Cars Transformed American
Freedom* (Cambridge, MA, and London, 2019).

30 "Officer Who Killed Minnesota Man in Front of Woman and
Child Identified," *Associated Press*, www.cbc.ca, July 7, 2016.

31 "Fatal Police Violence by Race and State in the USA, 1980–2019:
A Network Meta-Regression," *The Lancet*, 398 (2021), pp. 1239–55.

32 For an excellent assessment of these DOJ reform agreements:
J. Skinner, "An Evaluation of Department of Justice Agreements
in Large City Police Departments," PhD thesis, School of Public
Policy, University of Maryland, Baltimore County, 2021.

33 Devon W. Carbado, "From Stopping Black People to Killing Black
People: The Fourth Amendment Pathways to Police Violence,"
California Law Review, CV (2016), pp. 125–64.

34 R. Ray, "Bad Apples Come from Rotten Trees in Policing,"
Brookings, www.brookings.edu, May 30, 2020; C. M. Katz and
E. R. Maguire, *Transforming the Police: Thirteen Key Reforms* (Long
Grove, IL, 2022).

35 Kimbriell Kelly et al., "Fired/Rehired," *Washington Post*,
www.washingtonpost.com, August 17, 2017.

36 S. Rushin, "Federal Enforcement of Police Reform," *Fordham
Law Review*, LXXXII (2014).

37 K. Parker et al., "Amid Protest, Majorities Across Racial, Ethnic
Groups Express Support for the Black Lives Matter Movement,"
Pew Research Center, www.pewresearch.org, June 12, 2020.

38 E. G. Chueca and F. Tedoro, "Pandemic and Social Protests:
Cities as Flashpoints in the COVID-19 Era," *CIDOB*, www.cidob.org,
January 1, 2022.

39 "An After-Action Review of City Agencies' Responses to Activities
Directly Following George Floyd's Death on May 25, 2020," Final
Report, *City of Minneapolis*, https://lims.minneapolismn.gov,
March 7, 2022.

40 M. Berman, "Nearly Two Years after George Floyd's Death, Fallout
over Police Response to Unrest Continues," *Washington Post*, www.
washingtonpost.com, March 29, 2022.

41 See N. Hannah-Jones, *The 1619 Project: A New American Origin*
(New York, 2021).

42 See J. Karl, *Betrayal: The Final Act of the Trump Show* (New York,
2021), pp. 39, 49–50.

6 The Coup

1 "Record High Turnout in 2020 General Election," *United States
Census Bureau*, www.census.gov. The United States generally ranks
low in international comparisons of voting. In 2016 only 56 percent
of the eligible population voted. In Sweden, in contrast, it was

82 percent (2018) and 66 percent for Mexico (2018). D. Desilver, "Turnout in u.s Has Soared in Recent Elections but By some Measures Still Trails that of Many Other Countries," *Pew Research Center*, www.pewresearch.org, November 1, 2022.

2 Compare the 2020 one-page affirmation of support for Trump with the detailed 2016 platform. "Resolution Regarding the Republican Party Platform," *Republican National Committee*. See https://prod-cdn-static.gop.com/media.

3 It was moved to this date in 1937. If that date falls on a Sunday, the event is moved to the following Monday.

4 S. Boburg, "GOP Donor Described Botched Vote Fraud Probe in Recording, Prosecutors Say," *Washington Post*, www.washingtonpost.com, May 6, 2022.

5 Among the many good books on the final days of the Trump presidency see M. Bender, *Frankly, We Did Win This Election* (New York and Boston, MA, 2021); J. Karl, *Betrayal: The Final Act of the Trump Show* (New York, 2021); C. Leonning and P. Rucker, *I Alone Can Fix It: Donald J. Trump's Catastrophic Final Year* (New York, 2021); M. Wolff, *Landslide: The Final Days of the Trump Presidency* (New York, 2021); R. Woodward and R. Costa, *Peril* (New York, 2021).

6 R. Helderman et al., "New Evidence Shows Trump Was Told Many Times there Was No Voter Fraud—but He Kept Saying It," *Washington Post*, www.washingtonpost.com, March 3, 2022.

7 J. Mayer, "Legal Scholars Are Shocked by Ginni Thomas's 'Stop the Steal' Texts," *New Yorker*, www.newyorker.com, March 25, 2022.

8 M. Kranish, "Inside Mark Meadows's Final Push to Keep Trump in Power," *Washington Post*, www.washingtonpost.com, May 9, 2022.

9 C. Bethea, "Why Did Mark Meadows Register to Vote at an Address Where He Did Not Reside?" *New Yorker*, www.newyorker.com, March 6, 2022.

10 B. Reinhard et al., "As Giuliani Coordinated Plan for Trump Electoral Votes in States Biden Won, Some Electors Balked," *Washington Post*, www.washingtonpost.com, January 20, 2022.

11 K. Benner, "Trump and Justice Dept. Lawyer Said to Have Plotted to Oust Acting Attorney General," *New York Times*, www.nytimes.com, January 22, 2021.

12 M. Bowden and M. Teague, *The Steal: The Attempt to Overturn the 2020 Election and the People Who Stopped It* (New York, 2022).

13 M. Kranish, "Inside Ted Cruz's Last-Ditch Battle to Keep Trump in Power," *Washington Post*, www.washingtonpost.com, March 28, 2022.

14 M. Alfaro, "Lee Worked Hard to Overturn Election, Keep Trump in Power, Texts Show," *Washington Post*, www.washingtonpost.com, April 15, 2022.

15 J. Dawsey et al., "Memo Circulated among Trump Allies Advocated Using NSA Data in Attempt to Prove Stolen Election," *Washington Post*, www.washingtonpost.com, February 3, 2022.

16 C. Silverman et al., "Post-Vote Vitriol Surged in Groups on Facebook," *Washington Post*, www.washingtonpost.com, January 5, 2022.

17 T. Cotton, "Send in the Troops," *New York Times*, www.nytimes.com, June 3, 2020.

7 The Assault on the Capitol

1 C. Silverman, "Post-Vote Vitriol Surged in Groups on Facebook," *Washington Post*, www.washingtonpost.com, January 5, 2022.

2 D. Hakin and J. Becker, "The Long Crusade of Clarence and Ginni Thomas," *New York Times Magazine*, www.nytimes.com, September 1, 2022.

3 Quotes are taken from "Transcript of Trump's Speech at Rally before UC Capitol Riot," *AP News*, https://apnews.com, January 13, 2021.

4 "The Oath Keepers Militia Group's Path to Breaching the Capitol," *CBS News*, www.cbsnews.com, June 20, 2021.

5 Ibid.

6 S. Hsu, "Fla. Man Pleads Guilty in Jan. 6th Riot, Agrees to Cooperate," *Washington Post*, p. B5, June 24, 2021.

7 "Trump and Biden Discuss Portland Protest Violence, Proud Boys and Antifa during Presidential Debate," *YouTube*, www.youtube.com, September 29, 2020.

8 S. S. Hsu and T. Jakman, "First Jan 6 Defendant Convicted at Trial Receives Longest Sentence of 7 Years," *Washington Post*, www.washingtonpost.com, August 1, 2022.

9 M. Barkun, "Donald Trump and the Myth of the Deep State," in *Exposing the Right and Fighting for Democracy*, ed. P. Chamberlin et. al. (London, 2021), pp. 114–20. See also M. Barkun, "President Trump and the 'Fringe'," *Terrorism and Political Violence*, XXIX (2017), pp. 437–43.

10 "The Oath Keepers Militia Group's Path to Breaching the Capitol," www.youtube.com, accessed 28 May, 2023.

11 S. A. Sund, *Courage Under Fire: Under Siege and Outnumbered 58 to 1* (Ashland, OR, 2023).

12 S. Schneider, "The Far Right Embraces Violence Because It Has No Real Political Program," *Washington Post*, www.washingtonpost. com, January 15, 2021.

13 N. Fenno, "Inside Klete Keller's Fall from Olympic Gold to the Capitol Riot," *LA Times*, www.latimes.com, January 4, 2022.

14 S. S. Hsu, "Far-Right UCLA Student Who Sat in VP's Chair on Jan. 6 Pleads Guilty," *Washington Post*, www.washingtonpost.com, May 19, 2022.

15 Todd Frankel, "A Majority of People Arrested for Capitol Riot Had a History of Financial Trouble," www.washingtonpost.com, February 10, 2021.

16 P. Norris and R. Inglehart, *Cultural Backlash: Trump, Brexit, and Authoritarian Populism* (Cambridge, 2019).

17 S. Tobias and A. Stein, eds, *The Perils of Populism* (New Brunswick, NJ, 2022).

18 John Komlos, "A Revealing Look into the January 6th Insurrectionists," *DC Report*, www.dcreport.org, 2022.

8 Aftermath

1 M. Gerson, "A Fresh Start for Republicans can Come Only if They Abandon Authoritarian Populism," *Washington Post*, www. washingtonpost.com, January 18, 2022.

2 L. Cuthbert and A. Theodoridis, "Do Republicans Really Believe Trump Won the 2020 Election? Our Research Suggests that They Do," *Washington Post*, www.washingtonpost.com, January 7, 2022.

3 "Report of the Select Committee to Investigate the January 6th Attack on the United States Capitol," *United States House of Representatives*, www.house.gov, December 19, 2022.

4 R. Brownstein, "The Biggest Take Away from the January 6th Report," *The Atlantic*, https://apple.news, December 23, 2022.

5 M. Gerson, "A Man Who Contemplated a Military Coup Against the Constitution Is Approved of By More than 80 Percent of Republicans," *Washington Post*, www.washingtonpost.com, February 4, 2022.

6 C. Zakrzewski, C. Lima, and D. Harwell, "What the January 6 Probe Found Out about Social Media but Didn't Report," *Washington Post,* www.washingtonpost.com, January 17, 2023.

7 J. Lepore, "What the January 6th Report Is Missing," *New Yorker*, www.newyorker.com, January 16, 2023.

8 M. Barkun, "Conspiracy Theories as Stigmatized Knowledge," *Diogenes*, LXII (2015), pp. 114–20.

9 C. Miller-Idriss, *Hate in the Homeland* (Princeton, NJ, 2022).

10 A. Taub, "Counting Votes and Cutting Violence," *New York Times*, www.nytimes.com, February 22, 2023. The paper she draws upon is Camilo Nieto-Matiz and Natán Skigin, "Why Programmatic Parties Reduce Criminal Violence: Theory and Evidence from Brazil," *Research and Politics*, X/1 (2023).

11 A. Goldman, K. Benner, and Z. Kanno-Youngs, "How Trump's Focus on Antifa Distracted Attention from the Far Right Threat," *New York Times*, www.nytimes.com, 31 January 2021.

12 P. Wallach, "We Can Now Quantify Trump's Sabotage of the GOP House," *Washington Post*, www.washingtonpost.com, November 16, 2023.

13 I. Arnsdorf and M. Scherer, "Trump, Who as President Fermented an Insurrection, Says He Is Running Again," *Washington Post*, www.washingtonpost.com, November 15, 2022.

14 Tom Wolfe, *Mauve Gloves and Madmen, Clutter and Vine and Other Stories* (New York, 1976), p. 117.

15 See S. Levitsky and D. Ziblatt, *How Democracies Die* (New York, 2019).

16 See B. F. Walter, *How Civil Wars Start: And How to Stop Them* (New York, 2022).

Acknowledgments

It felt personal.

In January 2021 I had been living in Washington, DC, for almost ten years. I lived on 4th St. SE, little more than half a mile from the Capitol. During my time there, and especially during the COVID-19 lockdown, I would take walks and bicycle rides around the city in my eagerness to get out of the house. Lisa and I wandered all over but especially the area around Capitol Hill. It was our neighborhood, so the events of January 6 were all the more unsettling. They were not just events in a distant city, seen indirectly on a screen, but very disturbing events very close to home. This was especially the case when, after the insurrection, our neighborhood was transformed by barricades, armored vehicles, and the ubiquitous presence of armed military. The insurrection and its aftermath were together a deeply felt personal experience, and so my first acknowledgement is for the opportunity provided by living in the city at such a tumultuous time. The rising tension in the summer of 2020 was palpable in the militarization of DC. Living in the city at this time, so close to the Capitol, gave me a distinct vantage point to the events leading up to and after the insurrection.

I would also like to acknowledge the people at Reaktion. Michael Leaman, for enthusiastically accepting the book proposal, and my editor Amy Salter, and others for their great work in turning it into this finished product. I owe a debt to the eagle eyes of Ken Moxham, the proofreader who saved me from many errors and wayward passages.

Writing, and especially writing a book over a long period, is a very selfish pursuit, as too often more important things fly to the periphery. So, this is an inadequate thanks to Lisa for living with the obsessive writer that is her husband.